Treasure of Ambedkar Series 08

THE UNTOUCHABLES

Treasure of Ambedkar Series 08

THE UNTOUCHABLES

WHO WERE THEY AND WHY THEY BECAME UNTOUCHABLES?

Dr B.R. Ambedkar

KALPAZ

Treasure of Ambedkar Series 08

THE UNTOUCHABLES

ISBN: 978-93-5128-264-8

First Published 1948
Reprint **2017**, in India by
Kalpaz Publications
C-30, Satyawati Nagar,
Delhi – 110052
E-mail: kalpaz@hotmail.com
Ph.: 9212142040

Printed at: G. Print Process, Delhi

Inscribed to the memory of

NANDNAR

RAVIDAS

CHOKHAMELA

THREE RENOWNED SAINTS WHO WERE BORN AMONG THE UNTOUCHABLES AND WHO BY THEIR PIETY AND VIRTUE WON THE ESTEEM OF ALL

CONTENTS

PART V

The New Theories and some Hard Questions.

PART VI

Untouchability and the Date of its Birth.

PREFACE

This book is a sequel to my treatise called *The Shudras—Who they were and How they came to be the Fourth Varna of the Indo-Aryan Society* which was published in 1946. Besides the Shudras, the Hindu Civilization has produced three social classes whose existence has not received the attention it deserves. The three classes are :—

(*i*) The Criminal Tribes who number about 20 millions or so ;

(*ii*) The Aboriginal Tribes who number about 15 millions ; and

(*iii*) The Untouchables who number about 50 millions.

The existence of these classes is an abomination. The Hindu Civilization, gauged in the light of these social products, could hardly be called civilization. It is a diabolical contrivance to suppress and enslave humanity. Its proper name would be Infamy. What else can be said of a civilization which has produced a mass of people who are taught to accept crime as an approved means of earning their livelihood, another mass of people who are left to live in full bloom of their primitive barbarism in the midst of civilization and a third mass of people who are treated as an entity beyond human intercourse and whose mere touch is enough to cause pollution ?

In any other country the existence of these classes would have led to searching of the heart and to investigation of their origin. But neither of these has occured to the mind of the Hindu. The reason is simple. The Hindu does not regard the existence of these classes as a matter of apology or shame and feels no responsibility either to atone for it or to inquire into its origin and growth. On the other hand, every Hindu is taught to believe that his civilization is not only the most ancient but that it is also in many respects altogether unique. No Hindu ever feels tired of repeating these claims. That the Hindu Civilization is the most ancient, one can understand and even allow. But it is not quite so easy to understand on what grounds they rely for claiming that the Hindu Civilization is a unique one. The Hindus may not like it, but so far as it strikes non-Hindus, such a claim can rest only on one ground. It is the existence of these classes for which the Hindu Civilization is responsible. That the existence of such classes is a unique phenomenon, no Hindu need repeat, for nobody can deny the fact. One only wishes that the Hindu realized that it was a matter for which there was more cause for shame than pride.

The inculcation of these false beliefs in the sanity, superiority and sanctity of Hindu Civilization is due entirely to the peculiar social psychology of Hindu scholars.

To-day all scholarship is confined to the Brahmins. But unfortunately no Brahamin scholar has so far come forward to play the part of a Voltaire who had the intellectual honesty to rise against the doctrines of the Catholic Church in which he was brought up ; nor is one likely to appear on the scene in the future. It is a grave reflection on the scholarship of the Brahmins that they should not have produced a Voltaire. This will not cause surprise if it is remembered that the Brahmin scholar is only a learned man. He is not an intellectual There is a world of difference between one who is learned and one who is an intellectual. The former is class-conscious and is alive to the interests of his class. The latter is an emancipated being who is free to act without being swayed by class considerations. It is because the Brahmins have been only learned men that they have not produced a Voltaire.

Why have the Brahmins not produced a Voltaire ? The question can be answered only by another question. Why did the Sultan of Turkey not abolish the religion of the Mohammedan World ? Why has no Pope denounced

Catholicism? Why has the British Parliament not made a law ordering the killing of all blue-eyed babies? The reason why the Sultan or the Pope or the British Parliament has not done these things is the same as why the Brahmins have not been able to produce a Voltaire. It must be recognized that the selfish interest of a person or of the class to which he belongs always acts as an internal limitation which regulates the direction of his intellect. The power and position which the Brahmins possess is entirely due to the Hindu Civilization which treats them as supermen and subjects the lower classes to all sorts of disabilities so that they may never rise and challenge or threaten the superiority of the Brahmins over them. As is natural, every Brahmin is interested in the maintenance of Brahmanic supremacy be he orthodox or unorthodox, be he a priest or a *grahasta*, be he a scholar or not. How can the Brahmins afford to be Voltaires? A Voltaire among the Brahmins would be a positive danger to the maintenance of a civilization which is contrived to maintain Brahmanic supremacy. The point is that the intellect of a Brahmin scholar is severely limited by anxiety to preserve his interest. He suffers from this internal limitation as a result of which he does not allow his intellect full play which honesty and integrity demands. For, he fears that it may affect the interests of his class and therefore his own.

But what annoys one is the intolerance of the Brahmin scholar towards any attempt to expose the Brahmanic literature. He himself would not play the part of an iconoclast even where it is necessary. And he would not allow such non-Brahmins as have the capacity to do so to play it. If any non-Brahmin were to make such an attempt the Brahmin scholars would engage in a conspiracy of silence, take no notice of him, condemn him outright on some flimsy grounds or dub his work useless. As a writer engaged in the exposition of the Brahmanic literature I have been a victim of such mean tricks.

Notwithstanding the attitude of the Brahmin scholars, I must pursue the task I have undertaken.

For the origin of these classes is a subject which still awaits investigation. This book deals with one of these unfortunate classes namely, the Untouchables. The Untouchables are the most numerous of the three. Their existence is also the most unnatural. And yet there has so far been no investigation into their origin. That the Hindus should not have undertaken such an investigation is perfectly understandable. The old orthodox Hindu does not think that there is anything wrong in the observance of Untouchability. To him it is a normal and natural thing. As such it neither calls for expiation nor explanation. The new modern Hindu realizes the wrong. But he is ashamed to discuss it in public for fear of letting the foreigner know that Hindu Civilization can be guilty of such a vicious and infamous system or social code as evidenced by Untouchability. But what is strange is that Untouchability should have failed to attract the attention of the European student of social institutions. It is difficult to understand why. The fact, however, is there.

This book may, therefore, be taken as a pioneer attempt in the exploration of a field so completely neglected by everybody. The book, if I may say so, deals not only with every aspect of the main question set out for inquiry, namely, the origin of Untouchability, but it also deals with almost all questions connected with it. Some of the questions are such that very few people are even aware of them; and those who are aware of them are puzzled by them and do not know how to answer them. To mention only a few, the book deals with such questions as: Why do the Untouchables live outside the village? Why did beef-eating give rise to Untouchability? Did the Hindus never eat beef? Why did non-Brahmins give up beef-eating? What made the Brahmins become vegetarians, etc? To each one of these, the book suggests an answer. It may be that the answers given in the book to these questions are not all-embracing. Nonetheless it will be found that the book points to a new way of looking at old things.

The thesis on the origin of Untouchability advanced in the book is an altogether novel thesis. It comprises the following propositions :—

(1) There is no racial difference between the Hindus and the Untouchables;

(2) The distinction between the Hindus and Untouchables in its original form, before the advent of Untouchability, was the distinction between Tribesmen and Broken Men from alien Tribes. It is the Broken Men who subsequently came to be treated as Untouchables;

(3) Just as Untouchability has no racial basis so also has it no occupational basis;

(4) There are two roots from which Untouchability has sprung:

(*a*) Contempt and hatred of the Broken Men as of Buddhists by the Brahmins;

(*b*) Continuation of beef-eaing by the Broken Men after it had been given up by others.

(5) In searching for the origin of Untouchability care must be taken to distinguish the Untouchables from the Impure. All orthodox Hindu writers have identified the Impure with the Untouchables. This is an error. Untouchables are distinct from the Impure.

(6) While the Impure as a class came into existence at the time of the Dharma Sutras the Untouchables came into being much later than 400 A. D.

These conclusions are the result of such historical research as I have been able to make. The ideal which a historian should place before himself has been well defined by Goethe who said[1]:—

> "The historian's duty is to separate the true from the false, the certain from the uncertain, and the doubtful from that which cannot be accepted ... ... Every investigator must before all things look upon himself as one who

1. Maxims and Reflections of Goethe, Nos. 453, 543.

> is summoned to serve on a jury. He has only to consider how far the statement of the case is complete and clearly set forth by the evidence. Then he draws his conclusion and gives his vote, whether it be that his opinion coincides with that of the foreman or not."

There can be no difficulty in giving effect to Goethe's direction when the relevant and necessary facts are forthcoming. All this advice is of course very valuable and very necessary. But Goethe does not tell what the historian is to do when he comes across a missing link, when no direct evidence of connected relations between important events is available. I mention this because in the course of my investigations into the origin of Untouchability and other inter-connected problems I have been confronted with many missing links. It is true that I am not the only one who has been confronted with them. All students of ancient Indian history have had to face them. For as Mount Stuart Elphinstone has observed in Indian history "no *date* of a public event can be fixed before the invasion of Alexander; and no connected relation of the natural transactions can be attempted until after the Mohamedan conquest." This is a sad confession but that again does not help. The question is: "What is a student of history to do? Is he to cry halt and stop his work until the link is discovered?" I think not. I believe that in such cases it is permissible for him to use his imagination and intuition to bridge the gaps left in the chain of facts by links not yet discovered and to propound a working hypothesis suggesting how facts which cannot be connected by known facts might have been inter-connected. I must admit that rather than hold up the work, I have preferred to resort to this means to get over the difficulty created by the missing links which have come in my way.

Critics may use this weakness to condemn the thesis as violating the canons of historical research. If such be the attitude of the critics I must remind them that if there is a law which governs the evaluation of the results of historical results then refusal to accept a thesis on the ground that it is based on direct evidence is bad law. Instead of concentrating themselves on the issue of direct evidence *versus* inferential evidence and inferential evidence *versus* speculation, what the critics should concern themselves with is to examine (*i*) whether the thesis is based on pure conjecture, and (*ii*) whether the thesis is possible and if so does it fit in with facts better than mine does?

On the first issue I could say that the thesis would not be unsound merely because in some parts it is based on guess. My critics should remember that we are dealing with an institution the origin of which is lost in antiquity. The present attempt to explain the origin of Untouchability is not the same as writing history from texts which speak with certainty. It is a case of reconstructing history where there are no texts, and if there are, they have no direct bearing on the question. In such circumstances what one has to do is to strive to divine what the texts conceal or suggest without being even quite certain of having found the truth. The task is one of gathering survivals of the past, placing them together and making them tell the story of their birth. The task is analogous to that of the archaeologist who constructs a city from broken stones or of the palaeontologist who conceives an extinct animal from scattered bones and teeth or of a painter who reads the lines of the horizon and the smallest vestiges on the slopes of the hill to make up a scene. In this sense the book is a work of art even more than of history. The origin of Untouchability lies buried in a dead past which nobody knows. To make it alive is like an attempt to reclaim to history a city which has been dead since ages past and present it as it was in its original condition. It cannot but be that imagination and hypothesis should play a large part in such a work. But that in itself cannot be a ground for the condemnation of the thesis. For without trained imagination no scientific inquiry can be fruitful and hypothesis is the very soul of science. As Maxim Gorky has said[1]:

1. Literature and life. A selection from the writings of Maxim Gorky.

> "Science and literature have much in common; in both, observation, comparison and study are of fundamental importance; the artist like the scientist, needs both imagination and intuition. Imagination and intuition bridge the gaps in the chain of facts by its as yet undiscovered links and permit the scientist to create hypothesis and theories which more or less correctly and successfully direct the searching of the mind in its study of the forms and phenomenon of nature. They are of literary creation; the art of creating characters and types demands imagination, intuition, the ability to make things up in one's own mind".

It is therefore unnecessary for me to apologize for having resorted to constructing links where they were missing. Nor can my thesis be said to be vitiated on that account for nowhere is the construction of links based on pure conjecture. The thesis in great part is based on facts and inferences from facts. And where it is not based on facts or inferences from facts, it is based on circumstantial evidence of presumptive character resting on considerable degree of probability. There is nothing that I have urged in support of my thesis which I have asked my readers to accept on trust. I have at least shown that there exists a preponderance of probability in favour of what I have asserted. It would be nothing but pedantry to say that a preponderance of probability is not a sufficient basis for a valid decision.

On the second point with the examination of which, I said, my critics should concern themselves what I would like to say is that I am not so vain as to claim any finality for my thesis. I do not ask them to accept it as the last word. I do not wish to influence their judgement. They are of course free to come to their own conclusion. All I say to them is to consider whether this thesis is not a workable and therefore, for the time being, a valid hypothesis if the test of a valid hypothesis is that it should fit in with all surrounding facts, explain them and give them a meaning which in its absence they do not appear to have. I do not want anything more from my critics than a fair and unbiased appraisal.

January 1, 1948.
1, Hardinge Avenue,
New Delhi.

B. R. AMBEDKAR

PART I

A COMPARATIVE SURVEY.

CHAPTER I

Untouchability Among Non-Hindus

Who are the Untouchables and what is the origin of Untouchability? These are the main topics which it is sought to investigate and the results of which are contained in the following pages. Before launching upon the investigation it is necessary to deal with certain preliminary questions. The first such question is: Are the Hindus the only people in the world who observe Untouchability? The second is: If Untouchability is observed by Non-Hindus also how does Untouchability among Hindus compare with Untouchability among non-Hindus? Un fortunately no such comparative study has so far been attempted. The result is that though most people are aware of the existence of Untouchability among the Hindus they do not know what are its unique features. A definite idea of its unique and distinguishing features is however essential not merely for a real understanding of the position of the Untouchables but also as the best means of emphasising the need of investigating into their origin.

It is well to begin by examining how the matter stood in Primitive and Ancient Societies. Did they recognize Untouchability? At the outset it is necessary to have a clear idea as to what is meant by Untouchability. On this point, there can be no difference of opinion. It will be agreed on all hands that what underlies Untouchability is the notion of defilement, pollution, contamination and the ways and means of getting rid of that defilement.

Examining the social life of Primitive Society[1] in order to find out whether or not it recognized Untouchability in the sense mentioned above there can be no doubt that Primitive Society not only did believe in the notion of defilement but the belief had given rise to a live system of

1. The facts relating to pollution among non-Hindus are drawn from "Hastings Encyclopedia of Religion and Ethics", Vol. X, Article Purification, pp. 455-504.

well-defined body of rites and rituals.

Primitive Man believed that defilement was caused by

(1) the occurrences of certain events;

(2) contact with certain things; and

(3) contact with certain persons.

Primitive Men also believed in the transmission of evil from one person to another. To him the danger of such transmission was peculiarly acute at particular times such as the performance of natural functions, eating, drinking, etc. Among the events the occurrence of which was held by Primitive Man as certain to cause defilement were included the following:—

(1) Birth

(2) Initiation

(3) Puberty

(4) Marriage

(5) Cohabitation

(6) Death

Expectant mothers were regarded as impure and a source of defilement to others. The impurity of the mother extended to the child also.

Initiation and puberty are stages which mark the introduction of the male and the female to full sexual and social life. They were required to observe seclusion, a special diet, frequent ablutions, use of pigment for the body and bodily mutilation such as circumcision. Among the American Tribes not only did the initiates observe a special dietary but also took an emetic at regular intervals.

The ceremonies which accompanied marriage show that marriage was regarded by the Primitive Man as impure. In some cases the bride was required to undergo intercourse by men of the tribe as in Australia or by the chief or the medicine man of the tribe as in America or by the friends of the grooms as among the East African Tribes. In some cases there takes place the tapping of the bride by a sword by the bridegroom. In some cases, as among the Mundas, there takes place marriage to a tree before marriage with the bridegroom. All these marriage observances are intended to neutralize and prepare the individual against the impurity of marriage.

To the Primitive Man the worst form of pollution was death. Not only the corpse, but the possession of the belongings of the deceased were regarded as infected with pollution. The widespread custom of placing implements, weapons, etc., in the grave along with the corpse indicates that their use by others was regarded as dangerous and unlucky.

Turning to pollution arising out of contact with objects Primitive Man had learned to regard certain objects as sacred and certain others as profane. For a person to touch the sacred was to contaminate the sacred and to cause pollution to it. A most striking example of the separation of the sacred and the profane in Primitive Society is to be found among the Todas, the whole of whose elaborate ritual and (it would not be too much to say) the whole basis of whose social organisation is directed towards securing the ceremonial purity of the sacred herds, the sacred dairy, the vessels, and the milk, and of those whose duty it is to perform connected rites and rituals. In the dairy, the sacred vessels are always kept in a separate room and the milk reaches them only by transfer to and fro of an intermediate vessel kept in another room. The dairyman, who is also the priest, is admitted to office only after an elaborate ordination, which in effect is a purification. He is thereby removed from the rank of ordinary men to a state of fitness for sacred office. His conduct is governed by regulations such as those which permit him to sleep in the village and only at certain times, or that which entails that a dairyman who attends a funeral should cease from that time to perform his sacred function. It has, therefore, been conjectured that the aim of much of the ritual is to avert the dangers of profanation and prepare or neutralise the sacred substance for consumption by those who are themselves unclean.

The notion of the sacred was not necessarily confined to objects. There were certain classes of men who were sacred. For a person to touch them was to cause pollution. Among the Polynesians the tabu character of a Chief is violated by the touch of an inferior, although in this case the danger falls upon the inferior. On the other hand, in Efate the 'sacred man' who comes into contact with Namin (ceremonial uncleanliness) destroys his sacredness. In Uganda, before building a temple, the men were given four days in which to purify themselves. On the other hand, the Chief and his belongings are very often regarded as sacred and, therefore, as dangerous to others of an inferior rank. In the Tonga island, anyone who touches a Chief contacted tabu; it was removed by touching the sole of the foot of a superior chief. The sacred quality of the chief in Malaya Peninsula also resided in the Royal Regalia and anyone touching it was invited with serious illness or death.

Contact with strange people was also regarded as a source of Untouchability by the Primitive Man. Among the Bathonga, a tribe in South Africa, it is believed that those who travel outside their own country are peculiarly open to danger from the influence of foreign spirits and in particular from demoniac possession. Strangers are tabu because, worshipping strange gods, they bring strange influence with them. They are, therefore, fumigated or purified in some other way. In the Dieri and neighbouring tribes even a member of the tribe returning home after a journey was treated as a stranger and no notice was taken of him until he sat down.

The danger of entering a new country is as great as that which attaches to those who come from thence. In Australia, when one tribe approaches another, the members carry lighted sticks to purify the air, just as the Spartan kings in making war had sacred fires from the altar carried before them to the frontier.

In the same manner, those entering a house from the outside world were required to perform some ceremony, even if it were only to remove their shoes, which would purify the incomer from the evil with which otherwise he might contaminate those within, while the threshold, door-posts and lintel—important as points of contact with outer world—are smeared with blood or sprinkled with water when any member of household or of the community has become a source of pollution, or a horse-shoe is suspended over the door to keep out evil and bring goodluck.

Of course, the rites and ceremonies connected with birth, death, marriage, etc., do not positively and unequivocally suggest that they were regarded as sources of pollution But that pollution is one element among many others is indicated by the fact in every case there is segregation. There is segregation and isolation in birth, initiation, marriage, death and in dealing with the sacred and the strange.

In birth the mother is segregated. At puberty and initiation there is segregation and seclusion for a period. In marriage, from the time of betrothal until the actual ceremony bride and bride groom do not meet. In menstruation a woman is subjected to segregation. Segregation is most noticeable in the case of death. There is not only isolation of the dead-body but there is isolation of all the relatives of the dead from the rest of the community. This segregation is evidenced by the growth of hair and nail and wearing of old clothes by the relatives of the dead which show that they are not served by the rest of the society such as the barber, washerman, etc. The period of segregation and the range of segregation differ in the case of death but the fact of segregation is beyond dispute. In the case of defilement of the sacred by the profane or of defilement of the kindred or by intercourse with the non-kindred there is also the element of segregation. The profane must keep away from the sacred. So the kindred must keep away from the non-kindred. It is thus clear that in Primitive Society pollution involved segregation of the polluting agent.

Along with the development of the notion of defilement Primitive Society had developed certain purificatory media and purificatory ceremonies for dispelling impurity.

Among the agents used for dispelling impurity are water and blood. The sprinkling of water and the sprinkling of blood by the person defiled were enough to make him pure. Among purificatory rites were included changing of clothes, cutting hair, nail, etc., sweat-bath, fire, fumigation, burning of incense and fanning with the bough of a tree.

These were the means of removing impurity. But Primitive Society had another method of getting rid of impurity. This was to transfer it to another person. It was transferred to some one who was already tabu.

In New Zealand, if anyone touched the head of another, the head being a peculiarly 'sacred' part of the body, he became tabu. He purified himself by rubbing his hands on fernroot, which was then eaten by the head of the family in female line. In Tonga, if a man ate tabued food he saved himself from the evil consequences by having the foot of a chief placed on his stomach.

The idea of transmission also appears in the custom of the scapegoat. In Fiji, a tabued person wiped his hands on a pig, which became sacred to the chief, while in Uganda, at the end of the period of mourning for a king a 'scapegoat' along with a cow, a goat, a dog, a fowl and the dust and fire from the king's house was conveyed to the Bunyoro frontier, and there the animals were maimed and left to die. This practice was held to remove all uncleanliness from the king and queen.

Such are the facts relating to the notion of pollution as it prevailed in Primitive Society.

II

Turning to Ancient Society the notion of pollution prevalent therein was not materially different from what was prevalent in Primitive Society. There is difference as to the sources of pollution. There is difference regarding purificatory ceremonies. But barring these differences the pattern of pollution and purification in Primitive and Ancient Society is the same.

Comparing the Egyptian system of pollution with the Primitive system there is no difference except that in Egypt it was practised on an elaborate scale.

Among the Greeks the causes of impurity were bloodshed, the presence of ghost and contact with death, sexual intercourse, child-birth, the evacuation of the body, the eating of certain food such as pea-soup, cheese and garlic, the intrusion of unauthorised persons into holy places, and, in certain circumstances, foul speech and quarrelling. The purificatory means, usually called *kaopoia* by Greeks, were lustral water, sulphur, onions, fumigation and fire, incense, certain boughs and other vegetative growths, pitch, wool, certain stones and amulets, bright things like sunlight and gold, sacrificed animals, especially the pig and of these specially the blood and the skin; finally, certain festivals and festival rites particularly the ritual of cursing and the scapegoat. One unusual method was the cutting of the hair fo the polluted person or sacrificial communion with the deity.

A striking feature of the Roman notion of pollution and purification is to be found in the belief of territorial and communal pollution and purification. Parallel to the *lustratio* of the house is the periodical purifactory ritual applied to a country district (Pagi). The *lustractio pagi* consisted in a religious procession right round its boundaries, with sacrifice. There seems to have been in ancient days a similar procession round the walls of the city, called *amburbium*, In historical times special purification of the City was carried out when a calamity called for it, *e.g.* after the early disasters in the Second Punic War. The object of all such expiations was to seek reconciliation with the gods. Lustral ceremony accompanied the foundation of a colony. The *Therminalia* protective of boundaries, and the *Compitalia* of streets in the City were also probably lustral in their origin. Down to the late period, priests called *Luperci* perambulated in the boundaries of the earliest Rome, the settlement on the Palatinate. Earlier there was an annual solemn progress round the limits of the most ancient territory of the Primitive City. It was led by the Archaic priesthood called the *Arval* brotherhood. The ceremony was called *ambravalia* and it was distinctly piacular. When Roman territory was expanded no corresponding extension of the lustral rite seems ever to have been made. These round-about piacular surveys were common elsewhere, inside as well as outside Italy and particularly in Greece. The solemn words and prayers of the traditional chant, duly gone through without slip of tongue, seem to have had a sort of magical effect. Any error in the pronouncement of these forms would involve a need of reparation, just as in the earliest Roman legal system, the mispronounciation of the established verbal forms would bring loss of the lawsuit.

Other forms of quaint ancient ritual were connected with the piacular conception. The *Salii*, ancient priests of Mars, made a journey at certain times round a number of stations in the City. They also had a 'cleaning of the weapons' and a 'cleaning of the trumpets' which testify to a primitive notion that the efficiency of the army's weapons required purification. The 'washing' (lustrum) with which the census ended was in essence military; for it was connected with the *Comitia Centuriata*, which is merely the army in civil garb. *Lustratio exercitus* was often performed when the army was in the field, to remove superstitious dread which sometimes attacked it· at other times, it was merely prophylactic There was also a lustration of the fleet.

Like all Primitive people the Hebrews also entertained the notion of defilement. The special feature of their notion of defilement was the belief that defilement was also caused by contact with the carcass of unclean animals, by eating a carcass or by contact with creeping things, or by eating creeping things and by contact with animals which are always unclean such as "every beast which divideth the hoof, and is not cloven footed, nor cheweth the cud...whatsoever goeth upon his pawes, among all manner of beasts that go on all four". Contact with any unclean person was also defilement to the Hebrews. Two other special features of the Hebrew notion of defilement may be mentioned. The Hebrews believed that defilement might be caused to persons by idolatrous practices or to a land by the sexual impurities of the people.

On the basis of this survey, we can safely conclude that there are no people Primitive or Ancient who did not enterain the notion of pollution

CHAPTER II

Untouchability Among Hindus

In the matter of pollution there is nothing to distinguish the Hindus from the Primitive or Ancient peoples. That they recognized pollution is abundantly clear from the Manu Smriti. Manu recognises physical defilement and also notional defilement.

Manu treated birth,[1] death and menstruation[2] as sources of impurity; with regard to death, defilement was very extensive in its range. It followed the rule of consanguity. Death caused defilement to members of the family of the dead person technically called *Sapindas* and *Samanodakas*.[3] It not only included maternal relatives such as maternal uncle[4] but also remote relatives.[5] It extended even to non-relatives such as (1) teacher[6], (2) teacher's[7] son, (3) teacher's[8] wife, (4) pupil,[9] (5) fellow[10] student, (6) Shrotriya,[11] (7) king,[12] (8) friend,[13] (9) members of the household,[14] (10) those who carried the corpse,[15] and (11) those who touched the corpse.[16]

Anyone within the range of defilement could not escape it. There were only certain persons who were exempt. In the following verses Manu names them and specifies the reasons why he exempts them :—

"V. 93. The taint of impurity does not fall on kings

---

1. Chapter V. 58, 61—63,71,77,79.
2. " III, 45-46 ; IV 40-41,57,208 ; V. 66,85,108.
3. " V. 58,60, 75-77, 83-94.
4. " V. 81.
5. " V. 78.
6. " V. 65,80,82
7. " V. 80
8. " V. 80
9. " V. 81
10. " V. 71
11. " V. 81
12. " V. 82
13. " V. 82
14. " V. 81.
15. " V. 64-65, 85.
16. " V. 64,85.

and those engaged in the performance of a vow, or of a Sattra ; for the first are seated on the throne of India, and the (last two are) ever pure like Brahman.

94. For a king, on the throne of magnanimity, immediate purification is prescribed, and the reason for that is that he is seated (there) for the protection of (his) subjects.

95. (The same rule applies to the kinsmen) of those who have fallen in a riot or a battle, (of those who have been killed) by lightning or by the king, and for cows and Brahmins, and to those whom the king wishes to be pure (in spite of impurity),

96. A king is an incarnation of the eight guardian deities of the world, the Moon, the Fire, the Sun, the Wind, Indra, the Lords of wealth and water (Kubera and Varuna) and Yama.

97. Because the king is pervaded by those lords of the world, no impurity is ordained for him for purity and impurity of mortals is caused and removed by those lords of the world,"

From this it is clear that the king, the kinsmen of those who have fallen in a noble cause as defined by Manu and those whom the king chose to exempt were not affected by the normal rules of defilement. Manu's statement that the Brahmin was 'ever pure' must be understood in its usual sense of exhalting the Brahmin above everything. It must not be understood to mean that the Brahmin was free from defilement. For he was not. Indeed besides being defiled by births and deaths the Brahmin also suffered defilement on grounds which did not affect the Non-Brahmins. The Manu Smriti is full of tabus and don'ts which affect only the Brahmins and which he must observe and failure to observe which makes him impure.

The idea of defilement in Manu is real and not merely notional. For he makes the food offered by the polluted person unacceptable.

Manu also prescribes the period of defilement. It varies. For the death of a Sapinda it is ten days. For children three days. For fellow students one day. Defilement does not vanish by the mere lapse of the prescribed period. At the end of the period there must be performed a purificatory ceremony appropriate to the occasion.

For the purposes of purification Manu treats the subject of defilement from three aspects : (1) Physical defilement, (2) notional or psychological defilement, and (3) ethical defilement. The rule[1] for the purification of ethical defilement which occurs when a person entertains evil thoughts are more admonitions and exhortations. But the rites for the removal of notional and physical defilement are the same. They include the use of water,[2] earth,[3] cows urine,[4] the kusa grass[5] and ashes.[6] Earth, cow's urine, Kusa grass and ashes are prescribed as purifactory agents for removing physical impurities caused by the touch of inanimate objects. Water is the chief agent for the removal of notional defilement. It is used in three ways (1) sipping, (2) bath, and (3) ablution.[7] Later on *panchagavya* became the most important agency for removing notional defilement. It consists of a mixture of the five products of the cow, namely, milk, urine, dung, curds and butter.

In Manu there is also provision for getting rid of defilement by transmission through a scapegoat[8] namely by touching the cow or looking at the sun after sipping water.

Besides the individual pollution the Hindus believe also in territorial and communal pollution and purification very much like the system that prevailed among the early Romans. Every village has an annual *jatra*. An animal, generally a he-buffalo, is purchased on behalf of the village. The animal is taken round the village and is sacrificed, the blood is sprinkled round the village and towards the end toe meat is distributed among the villagers. Every Hindu, every Brahmin even though he may not be a beef eater is bound to

1. Chapter V. 105-109; 127-128.
2. „ V. 127.
3. „ V. 134-136.
4. „ V. 121, 124.
5. „ V. 115.
6. „ V. 111.
7. „ V. 143.
8. „ V. 87.

accept his share of the meat. This is not mentioned in any of the Smritis but it has the sanction of custom which among the Hindus is so strong that it always overrides law.

II

If one could stop here, one could well say that the notion of defilement prevalent among the Hindus is not different from that which obtained in Primitive and in Ancient Societies. But one cannot stop here. For there is another form of Untouchability observed by the Hindus which has not yet been set out. It is the hereditary Untouchability of certain communities. So vast is the list of such communities that it would be difficult for an individual with his unaided effort to compile an exhaustive list. Fortunately such a list was prepared by the Government of India in 1935 and is attached to the Orders-in-Council issued under the Government of India Act of 1935. To this Order-in-Council there is attached a Schedule. The Schedule is divided into nine parts. One part refers to one province and enumerates the castes, races or tribes or parts of or groups within steps which are deemed to be Untouchables in that province either in the whole of that province or part thereof. The list may be taken to be both exhaustive and authentic. To give an idea of the vast number of communities which are regarded as hereditary Untouchables by the Hindus, I reproduce below the list given in the Order-in-Council.

SCHEDULE

PART I.—MADRAS

(1) Scheduled Castes throughout the Province :—

Adi-Andhra.
Adi-Dravida.
Adi-Karnataka.
Ajila.
Arunthuthiyar.
Baira.
Bakuda.
Bandi.
Bariki.
Battada.
Bavuri.
Bellara.
Byagari
Chachati.
Chakkiliyan.
Chalavadi.
Chamar.
Chandala.
Cheruman.
Dandasi.
Devendrakulathan.
Ghasi.
Godagali.
Godari.
Godda.
Gosangi.
Haddi
Hasla.
Holeya.
Jaggali.
Jambuvulu.
Kalladi.
Kanakkan.
Kodalo.
Koosa.
Koraga.
Kudumbas.
Kuravan.
Madari.

Madiga.
Maila.
Mala.
Mala Dasu.
Matangi.
Moger.
Muchi.
Mundala.
Nalakeyava.
Nayadi.
Paga dai.
Paidi.
Painda.
Paky.
Pallan.
Pambada.
Pamidi.
Panchama.
Paniyan.
Panniandi
Paraiyan.
Paravan.
Pulayan.
Puthirai Vannan.
Raneyar.
Relli.
Samagara.
Samban.
Sapari.
Semman.
Thoti.
Tiruvalluvar.
Valluvan.
Valmiki.
Vettuvan.

(2) Scheduled Castes throughout the Provinces except in any special constituency constituted under the Government of India Act, 1935, for the election of a representative of backward areas and backward tribes to the Legislative Assembly of the Province :—

Arnadan.
Dombo.
Kadan.
Karimpalan.
Kattunayakan.
Kudiya.
Kudubi.
Kurichchan.
Kuruman.
Malasar.
Mavilan.
Pano.

PART II.—BOMBAY

Scheduled Castes :—

(1) Throughout the Province :—

Asodi.
Bakad.
Bhambi.
Bhangi.
Chakrawadya-Dasar.
Chalvadi.
Chambhar, or Mochigar, or Samagar.
Chena-Dasaru.
Chuhar, or Chuhra.
Dakaleru.
Dhed.
Dhor.
Garode.
Halleer.
Halsar, or Haslar.
Hulsavar.
Holaya.
Khalpa.
Kolcha, or Kolgha.
Koli-Dhor.
Lingader.
Madig, or Mang.
Mahar.
MangGarudi.
Maghval, or Menghwar.
Mini Madig.
Mukri.
Nadia.
Shenva, or Shindhava.
Shinghdav, or Shingadya
Sochi.
Timali.
Turi.
Vankar.
Vitholia.

(2) Throughout the Province except in the Ahmedabad, Kaira, Broach and Panch Mahals and Surat Districts—Mochi.

(3) In the Kanara district—Kotegar.

PART III.—BENGAL

Scheduled Castes throughout the Province :—

Agaria.
Bagdi.
Bahelia.
Baiti.
Bauri.
Bediya.

Beldar.
Berua.
Bhatiya.
Bhuimali.
Bhuiya.
Bhumij.
Bind.
Binjhia.
Chamar.
Dhenuar.
Dhoba.
Doai.
Dom.
Dosadh.
Garo.
Ghasi.
Gonrhi.
Hadi.
Hajang.
Halalkhor.
Hari
Ho.
Jalia Kaibartta.
Jhalo Malo, or Malo.
Kadar.
Kalpahariya.
Kan.
Kandh.
Kandra.
Kaora.
Kapuria.
Karenga.
Kastha.
Kaur.
Khaira.
Khatik.
Koch.
Konai.
Konwar.
Kora.
Kotal.
Lalbegi.
Lodha.
Lahor.
Mahli.
Mal.
Mahar.
Mallah.
Mech.
Mehtor.
Muchi.
Munda.
Musahar.
Nagesia.
Namasudra.
Nat.
Nuniya.
Oraon.
Paliya.
Pan.
Pasi.
Patni.
Pod.
Rabha.
Rajbanshi.
Rajwar.
Santal.
Sunri.
Tiyar.
Turi.

PART IV.—UNITED PROVINCES

Scheduled Castes :—

(1) Throughout the Province:—

Agariva.
Aheriya.
Badi.
Badhik.
Baheliya.
Bajaniya.
Bajgi.
Balahar.
Balmiki.
Banmanus.
Bansphor.
Barwar.
Basor.
Bawariya.
Beldar.
Bengali.
Berya.
Bhantu.
Bhuiya.
Bhuiyar.
Boriya.
Chamar.
Chero.
Dabagar.
Dhangar.
Dhanuk (Bhangi).
Dharkar.
Dhobi.
Dom.
Domar.
Gharami.
Ghasiya.
Gual.
Habura.
Hari.
Hela.
Khairaha.
Kalabaz.
Kanjar.
Kapariya.
Karwal.
Kharot.
Kharwar (except Benbansi)
Khatik.
Kol.
Korwa.
Lalbegi.
Majhwar.
Nat.
Pankha.
Parahiya.
Pasi.
Patari.
Rawat.
Saharya.
Sanaurhiya.
Sansiya.

Shilpkar. Turaiha.
Tharu.

(2) Throughout the Province except in the Agra, Meerut and Rohilkhand divisions—Kori.

PART V.—PUNJAB

Scheduled Castes throughout the Province :—

Ad Dharmis.	Marija, or Marecha.	Khatik.
Bawaria.	Bengali.	Kori.
Chamar.	Barar.	Nat.
Chuhra, or Balmiki.	Bazigar.	Pasi.
Dagi and Koli.	Bhanjra.	Perna.
Dumna.	Chanal.	Sapela.
Od.	Dhanak.	Sirkiband,
Sansi.	Gagra.	Meghs.
Sarera.	Gandhila.	Ramdasis.

PART VI.—BIHAR

Scheduled Castes :—

(1) Throughout the Province :—

Chamar.	Halalkhor.	Mochi.
Chaupal.	Hari.	Musahar.
Dhobi.	Kanjar.	Nat.
Dusadh.	Kurariar.	Pasi.
Dom.	Lalbegi.	

(2) In the Patna and Tirhut divisions and the Bhagalpur, Monghyr, Palamau and Purnea districts :—

Bauri.	Bhumij.	Rajwar.
Bhogta.	Ghasi.	Turi.
Bhuiya.	Pan.	

(3) In the Dhanbad sub-division of the Manbhum district and the Central Manbhum general rural constituency, and the Purulia and Raghunathpur municipalities :—

Bauri.	Ghasi.	Rajwar.
Bhogta.	Pan.	Turi.
Bhuiya.		

PART VII.—CENTRAL PROVINCES AND BERAR

Scheduled Castes	*Localities*
Basor, or Burud	Throughout the Province.
Chamar	
Dom	
Ganda	
Mang	
Mehtar or Bhangi	
Mochi	
Satnami	

Scheduled Castes	*Localities*
Audhelia	In the Bilaspur district.
Bahna	In the Amraoti district.
Balahi, or Balai ...	In the Berar division and the Balaghat, Bhandara, Betul, Chanda, Chhindwara, Hoshangabad, Jubbulpore, Mandla, Nagpur, Nimar, Saugor and Wardha districts.
Bedar	In the Akola, Amroati, and Buldana districts.
Chadar	In the Bhandara and Saugor districts.
Chauhan	In the Drug district.
Dahayat	In the Damoh sub-division of the Saugor district.
Dewar	In the Bilaspur, Drug and Raipur districts.
Dhanuk	In the Saugor district, except in the Damoh sub-division thereof.
Dhimar	In the Bhandara district.
Dhobi	In the Bhandara, Bilaspur, Raipur and Saugor districts, and the Hoshangabad and Seoni-Malwa tahsils of the Hoshangabad district.
Dohor ...	In the Berar division and the Balaghat, Bhandara, Chanda, Nagpur and Wardha districts.
Ghasia	In the Berar division and in the Balaghat, Bhandara, Bilaspur, Chanda, Drug, Nagpur, Raipur and Wardha districts.
Holiya	In the Balaghat and Bhandara districts.
Jangam	In the Bhandara district.
Kaikari ...	In the Berar division, and in Bhandara, Chanda, Nagpur and Wardha districts.
Katia	In the Berar division, in the Balaghat, Betul, Bhandara, Bilaspur, Chanda, Drug, Nagpur, Nimar, Raipur and Wardha districts, in the Hoshangabad and Seoni-Malwa tahsils of the Hoshangabad district, in the Chhindwara district, except in the Seoni sub-division thereof, and in the Saugor district, except in the Damoh sub-division thereof.
Khangar	In the Bhandara, Buldana and Saugor districts and the Hoshangabad and Seoni Malwa tahsils of the Hoshangabad district.
Khatik	In the Berar division, in the Balaghat, Bhandara, Chanda, Nagpur and Wardha districts, in the Hoshangabad tahsil of the Hoshangabad district, in the Chhindwara district, except in the Seoni sub-division thereof, and in the Saugor district, except in the Damoh sub-division thereof.
Koli	In the Bhandara and Chanda districts.
Kori	In the Amraoti, Balaghat, Betul, Bhandara, Buldana, Chhindwara, Jubbulpore, Mandla Nimar, Raipur and Saugor districts, and in,

Scheduled Castes	*Localities*
	the Hoshangabad district, except in the Harda and Sohagpur tahsils thereof.
Kumhar	In the Bhandara and Saugor districts and the Hoshangabad and Seoni-Malwa tahsils of the Hoshangabad district.
Madgi	In the Berar division and in the Balaghat, Bhandara Chanda, Nagpur and Wardha districts.
Mala	In the Balaghat, Betul, Chhindwara, Hoshangabad, Jubbulpore Mandla, Nimar and Saugor districts.
Mehra, or Mahar ...	Throughout the Province, except in the Harda and Sohagpur tahsils of the Hoshangabad district.
Nagarchi	In the Balaghat, Bhandara, Chhindwara, Mandla, Nagpur and Raipur districts.
Ojha	In the Balaghat, Bhandara and Mandla districts and the Hoshangabad tahsil of the Hoshangabad district.
Panka	In the Berar division, in the Balaghat, Bhandara, Bilaspur, Chanda, Drug, Nagpur, Raipur, Saugor and Wardha districts and in the Chhindwara district, except in the Seoni sub-division thereof.
Pardhi	In the Narsinghpura sub-division of the Hoshangabad district.
Pradhan	In the Berar division, in the Bhandara, Chanda, Nagpur, Nimar, Raipur and Wardha districts and in the Chhindwara district, except in the Seoni sub-division thereof.
Rujjhar	In the Sohagpur tahsil of the Hoshangabad district.

PART VIII.—ASSAM

Scheduled Castes :—

(1) In the Assam Valley :—

Namasudra.
Kaibartta.
Bania, or Brittial-Bania.
Hira.
Lalbegi.
Mehtar, or Bhangi.
Bansphor.

(2) In the Surma Valley :—

Mali, or Bhuimali.
Dhupi, or Dhobi.
Dugla, or Dholi.
Jhalo and Malo.
Mahara.
Sutradhar.
Muchi.
Patni.
Namasudra.
Kaibartta, or Jaliya.
Lalbegi.
Mehtar, or Bhangi.
Bansphor.

PART IX.—ORISSA

Scheduled Castes :—

(1) Throughout the Province :—

Adi-Andhra.
Audhelia.
Bariki.
Basor, or Burud.
Bavuri.
Chachati.
Chamar.
Chandala.
Dandasi.
Dewar.
Dhoba or Dhobi.
Ganda.
Ghusuria.
Godagali.
Godari.
Godra.
Gokha.
Haddi, or Hari.
Irika.
Jaggali.
Kandra.
Katia.
Kela.
Kodalo.
Madari.
Madiga.
Mahuria.
Mala.
Mang.
Mangan.
Mehra, or Mahar,
Mehtar. or Bhangi.
Mochi, or Muchi.
Paidi.
Painda.
Pamidi.
Panchama.
Panka.
Relli.
Sapari.
Satnami.
Siyal.
Valmiki.

(2) Throughout the Province except in the Khondmals district, the district of Sambalpur and the areas transferred to Orissa under the provisions of the Government of India (Constitution of Orissa) Order, 1936, from the Vizagapatam and Ganjam Agencies in the Presidency of Madras :—

Pan, or Pano.

(3) Throughout the Province except in the Khondmals district and the areas so transferred to Orissa from the said Agencies :—

Dom, or Dambo.

(4) Throughout the Province except in the district of Sambalpur :—

Bauro,
Bhuiya.
Bhumij.
Ghasi, or Ghasia.
Turi.

(5) In the Nawapara sub-division of the district of Sambalpur :—

Kori.
Nagarchi.
Pradhan.

This is a very terrifying list. It includes 429 communities. Reduced to numbers it means that today there exist in India 50-60 millions of people whose mere touch causes pollution to the Hindus. Surely, the phenomenon of Untouchability among primitive and ancient society pales into insignificance before this phenomenon of hereditary

Untouchability for so many millions of people which we find in India. This type of Untouchability among Hindus stands in a class by itself. It has no parallel in the history of the world. It is unparalleled not merely by reason of the colossal numbers involved which exceed the number of great many nations in Asia and in Europe but also on other grounds.

There are some striking features of the Hindu system of Untouchability affecting the 429 Untochable communities which are not to be found in the custom of Untochability as observed by Non-Hindu communities, primitive or ancient.

The isolation prescribed by Non-Hindu societies as a safeguard against defilement, if it is not rational, is at least understandable. It is for specified reasons such as birth, marriage, death, etc. But the isolation prescribed by Hindu society is apparently for no cause.

Defilement as observed by the Primitive Society was of a temporary duration which arose during particular times such as the performance of natural functions, eating, drinking, etc., or a natural crisis in the life of the individual such as birth, death, menstruation, etc. After the period of defilement was over and after the purifactory ceremonies were performed the defilement vanished and the individual became pure and associable. But the impurity of the 50-60 millions of the Untouchables of India, quite unlike the impurity arising from birth, death, etc., is permanent. The Hindus who touch them and become polluted thereby can become pure by undergoing purifactory ceremonies. But there is nothing which can make the Untouchables pure. They are born impure, they are impure while they live, they die the death of the impure, and they give birth to children who are born with the stigma of Untouchability affixed to them. It is a case of permanent, hereditary stain which nothing can cleanse.

In the third place, Non-Hindu societies which believed in defilement isolated the individuals affected or at the most those closely connected with them. But the Untouchability among the Hindus involves the isolation of a class—a class which today numbers about 50 to 60 million people.

In the fourth place, Non-Hindu societies only *isolated* the affected individuals. They did not *segregate* them in separate quarters. The Hindu society insists on segregation of the Untouchables. The Hindu will not live in the quarters of the Untouchables and will not allow the Untouchables to live inside Hindu quarters. This is a fundamental feature of Untouchability as it is practised by the Hindus. It is not a case of social separation, a mere stoppage of social intercourse for a temporary period. It is a case of territorial segregation and of a *cordon sanitaire* putting the impure people inside a barbed wire into a sort of a cage. Every Hindu village has a ghetto. The Hindus live in the village and the Untouchables in the ghetto.

Such is the Hindu system of Untouchability. Who can deny that it is not altogether different from what is found to exist among Non-Hindu societies? That Untouchability among Hindus is a unique phenomenon is beyond question. Persons were treated by non-Hindu communities as impure but as individuals. Never a whole class was treated as impure. But their impurity was of a temporary duration and was curable by the performance of some purifactory rites. There has never been a case of permanent impurity based on the rule 'once impure always impure'. Persons were treated as impure by Non-Hindu Communities and they were even cut off from social intercourse. But there has never been a case of persons having been put into permanent segregation camps. A whole body of people have been treated as impure by Non-Hindu communities. But they were strangers outside the fold of the kindred. There has never been a case of a people treating a section of their own people as permanently and hereditarily impure.

Untouchability among Hindus is thus a unique phenomenon, unknown to humanity in other parts of the world. Nothing like it is to be found in any other society — primitive, ancient or modern. The many problems that arise out of a study of Untouchability and which call for investigation may be reduced to two :

(1) Why do the Untouchables live outside the village ?

(2) What made their impurity permanent, and ineradicable ?

The following pages are devoted to finding answers to these two questions.

PART II

PROBLEM OF HABITAT

Chapter III—Why do the Untouchables live outside the village ?
Chapter IV—Are the Untouchables Broken Men ?
Chapter V—Are there Parallel cases ?
Chapter VI—How did Separate Settlements for Broken Men disappear elsewhere ?

CHAPTER III

Why Do the Untouchables Live Outside the Village?

That the Untouchables live outside the village is so notorious a fact that it must be taken to be within the cognizance even of those whose knowledge about them is not very profound. Yet, nobody has thought that this was a serious question calling for satisfactory answer. How did the Untouchables come to live outside the village? Were they declared to be Untouchables first and then deported out of the village and made to live outside? Or were they from the very beginning living outside the village and were subsequently declared to be Untouchables? If the answer is that they were living outside the village from the very beginning, there arises a further question, namely, what can be the reason for it?

As the question of the separate settlement of the Untouchables has never been raised before, naturally there exists no theory as to how the Untouchables came to live outside the village. There is, of course, the view of the Hindu Shastras and if one wants to dignify it by calling it a theory one may do so. The Shastras of course say that the *Antyajas* should live and have their abode outside the village. For instance, Manu says:

"*X. 51.* But the dwellings of the *Chandalas* and the *Shvapakas* shall be outside the village, they must be made *Apapatras* and their wealth (shall be) dogs and donkeys.

X. 52. Their dress (shall be) the garments of the dead (they shall eat) their food from broken dishes, black iron (shall be) their ornaments and they must always wander from place to place.

X. 53. A man who fulfils a religious duty, shall not seek intercourse with them; their transactions (shall be) among themselves and their marriages with their equals.

X. 54. Their food shall be given to them by others (than an Aryan giver) in a broken dish; at night they shall not walk about in village and in towns.

X. 55. By day they may go about for the purpose of their work, distinguished by marks at king's command, and they shall carry out the corpses (of persons) who have no relatives; that is a settled rule.

X. 56. By the King's order they shall always execute the criminals, in accordance with the law, and they shall take for themselves the clothes, the beds, and the ornaments of (such) criminals."

But what conclusion can one draw from these statements of the Shastras? They are capable of double interpretation. When the Shastras say that the Untouchables should stay outside the village, they may be purporting to say no more than that the Untouchables should stay where they have been staying, i.e. outside the village. This is one interpretation. The second interpretation is that those who are declared Untouchables should not be allowed to stay inside the village but should be required to go out of the village and live outside. Following up the alternate interpretations of the Shastras there are two different possibilities which call for consideration. One is that the Untouchability has nothing to do with the Untouchables living outside the village. From the very beginning they lived outside the village. Thereafter when the stigma of Untouchability fell on them they were prohibited from coming to live inside the village. The other possibility is that Untouchability has everything to do with the Untouchables, living outside the village. In other words, the Untouchables originally lived inside the village and that thereafter when the stigma of untouchability fell on them they were forced to vacate and live outside the village.

Which of the two possibilities is more acceptable?

The second possibility is on the face of it absurd and fantastic. One argument is quite enough to expose its absurdity. The phenomenon we are discussing is not confined to a single village or single area. It exists all over India. The transplantation of the Untouchables from within the village to outside the village is a vast operation. How and who could have carried on an operation of such colossal dimensions? It could not have been carried out except by the command of an Emperor having his sway over the whole of India. Even to him such a transplantation would have been impossible. But possible and impossible it can only be the work of an Emperor. Who is the Emperor to whom the credit or discredit of this task can be assigned? Obviously, India had no Emperor to perform this task. If there was no Emperor to do the transplantation, then the second possibility must be abandoned.

That those who are called Untouchables lived outside the village from the very beginning even before they became Untouchables and that they continued to live outside the village because of the supervention of untouchability at a later stage is the only possibility worth consideration. But this raises a very difficult question: Why did they live outside the village? What made them or forced them to do so? The answer is that having regard to the factors which are known to students of Sociology to have influenced the transformation of Primitive Society into Modern Society all over the world it is only natural to suppose that the Untouchables should have from the beginning lived outside the village.

Not many will realise why this is natural without some explanation of the factors which have affected the condition of Primitive Society into Modern Society. For a clear understanding of the matter it is necessary to bear in mind that Modern Society differs from Primitive Society in two respects. Primitive Society consisted of nomadic communities while Modern Society consists of settled communities. Secondly, Primitive Society consisted of tribal communities based on blood relationship. Modern Society consists of local communities based on territorial affiliation. In other words there are two lines of evolution along which Primitive Society has proceeded before it became transformed into Modern Society. One line of evolution has led the Primitive Society to become a territorial community from being a tribal community. There can be no doubt that such a change has taken place. Clear traces of the change are to be seen in the official style of kings. Take the style of the English kings. King John was the first to call himself the king of England. His predecessors commonly called themselves kings of the English. The former represent a territorial community. The latter represent a tribal community. England was once the country which Englishmen inhabited. Englishmen are now the people who inhabit England. The same transformation can be seen to have taken place in the style of the French kings who were once called kings of the Franks and later as kings of France. The second line of evolution had led Primitive Society to become a settled community instead of the Nomadic community which it was. Here again, the change is so definite and so impressive that no illustration is required to convince anybody of its reality.

For the purpose in hand all we need is to confine ourselves to a consideration of the second line of evolution. How did Primitive Society become a settled community? The story of how Primitive Society became a settled community is too long to be detailed in a chapter—much too long to be compressed in a section thereof. It is enough to note two things. The first thing to understand is what made Primitive Society give up its nomadic life and secondly what happened in the transition from nomadic to settled life.

Primitive Society was no doubt nomadic. But it was nomadic not because of any migratory instinct. Nor was it due to any mental trait peculiar to it. It was the result of the fact that the earliest form of the wealth held by Primitive Society was cattle. Primitive Society was migratory because its wealth, namely the cattle, was migratory. Cattle went after new pastures. Primitive Society by reason of its love for cattle, therefore, went wherever its cattle carried it. Primitive Society became fixed in its abode, in other words became a settledcommunity, when a new species of wealth was discovered. This new species of wealth was land. This happened when Primitive Society learned the art of farming and of cultivating land. Wealth became fixed at one place when it changed its form from cattle to land. With this change Primitive Society also becamesettled at the same place.

This explains why Primitive Society was at one time nomadic and what led it take to settled life.

The next thing is to note the events that have happened when Primitive Society was on the road to becoming a Settled Society. The problems which faced Primitive Society in its tranition from Nomadic life to Settled life were mainly two. One confronted the Settled commvnity. The other confronted the

Broken men. The problem that confronted the Settled community was that of its defence against the Nomadic tribes. The problem which confronted the Broken men was that of the protection and shelter. It may be desirable to elucidate how and why these problems arose.

For an understanding of the problem which confronted the Settled tribes, it is necessary to bear in mind the following facts. All tribes did not take to settled life at one and the same time. Some became settled and some remained nomadic. The second thing to remember is that the tribes were never at peace with one another. They were always at war. When all tribes were in a Nomadic state the chief causes for intra-tribal warfare were (1) stealing cattle, (2) stealing women, and (3) stealthily grazing of cattle in the pastures belonging to other tribes. When some tribes became settled the tribes that remained nomadic found it more advantageous to concentrate their fight against the settled tribes. It was more paying than a war against other Nomadic tribes. The Nomadic tribes had come to realize that the Settled tribes were doubly wealthy. Like the Nomadic tribes, they had cattle. But in addition to cattle, they had corn which the Nomadic tribes had not and which they greatly coveted. The Nomadic tribes systematically organized raids on the Settled tribes with the object of stealing the wealth belonging to the Settled tribes. The third fact is that the Settled tribes were greatly handicapped in defending themselves against these raiders. Being engaged in more gainful occupation, the Settled tribes could not always convert their ploughs into swords. Nor could they leave their homes and go in pursuit of the raiding tribes. There is nothing strange in this. History shows that peoples with civilization but no means of defence are not able to withstand the attacks of the barbarians. This explains how and why during the transition period the Settled tribes were faced with the problem of their defence.

How the problem of the Broken men arose is not difficult to understand. It is the result of the continuous tribal warfare which was the normal life of the tribes in their primitive condition. In a tribal war it often happened that a tribe instead of being completely annihilated was defeated and routed. In many cases a defeated tribe became broken into bits. As a consequence of this there always existed in Primitive times a floating population consisting of groups of Broken tribesmen roaming in all directions. To understand what gave rise to the problem of the Broken men it is necessary to realize that Primitive Society was fundamentally tribal in its organization. That Primitive Society was fundamentally tribal meant two things. Firstly, every individual in Primitive Society belonged to a tribe. Nay, he must belong to the tribe. Outside the tribe no individual had any existence. He could have none. Secondly, tribal organization being based on common blood and common kinship an individual born in one tribe could not join another tribe and become a member of it. The Broken Men had, therefore, to live as stray individuals. In Primitive Society where tribe was fighting against tribe a stray collection of Broken Men was always in danger of being attacked. They did not know where to go for shelter. They did not know who would attack them and to whom they could go for protection. That is why shelter and protection became the problem of the Broken Men.

The foregoing summary of the evolution of Primitive Society shows that there was a time in the life of Primitive Society when there existed two groups — one group consisting of Settled tribes faced with the problem of finding a body of men who would do the work of watch and ward against the raiders belonging to Nomadic tribes and the other group consisting of Broken Men from defeated tribes with the problem of finding patrons who would give them food and shelter.

The next question is : How did these two groups solve their problems? Although we have no written text of a contract coming down to us from antiquity we can say that the two struck a bargain whereby the Broken Men agreed to do the work of watch and ward for the Settled tribes and the Settled tribes agreed to give them food and shelter. Indeed, it would have been unnatural if such an arrangement had not been made between the two especially when the interest of the one required the co-operation of the other.

One difficulty, however, must have arisen in the completion of the bargain, that of shelter. Where were the Broken Men to live? In the midst of the settled community or outside the Settled community? In deciding this question two considerations must have played a decisive part. One consideration is that of blood relationship. The second consideration is that of strategy. According to Primitive notions only persons of the same tribe, i. e. of the same blood, could live together. An alien could not be admitted inside the area occupied by the homesteads belonging to the tribe. The Broken men were aliens. They belonged to a tribe which was different from the Settled tribe. That being so, they could not be permitted to live in the midst of the Settled tribe. From the strategic point of view also it was desirable that these Broken men should live on the border of the village so as to meet the raids of the hostile tribes. Both these considerations were decisive in favour of placing their quarters outside the village.

We can now return to the main question, namely, why do the Untouchables live outside the village? The answer to the question can be sought along the lines indicated above. The same processes must have taken place in India when the Hindu Society was passing from Nomadic life to the life of a settled village community. There must have been in Primitive Hindu society, Settled tribes and Broken Men. The Settled tribes founded the village and formed the village community and the Broken Men lived in separate quarters outside the village for the reason that they belonged to a different tribe and, therefore, to different blood. To put it definitely, the Untouchables were originally only Broken Men. It is because they were Broken Men that they lived outside the village.

This explains why it is natural to suppose that the Untouchables from the very beginning lived outside and that Untouchability has nothing to do with their living outside the village.

The theory is so novel that critics may not feel satisfied without further questioning. They will ask:

(1) Is there any factual evidence to suggest that the Untouchables are Broken Men ?

(2) Is there evidence that the process of settlement suggested above has actually taken place in any country ?

(3) If Broken Men living outside the village is a universal feature of all societies, how is it that the separate quarters of the Broken Men have disappeared outside India but not in India ?

CHAPTER IV

Are the Untouchables Broken Men ?

To the question Are the Untouchables in their origin only Broken Men, my answer is in the affirmative. An affirmative answer is bound to be followed by a call for evidence. Direct evidence on this issue could be had if the totems of the Touchables and the Untouchables in the Hindu villages had been studied. Unfortunately the study of the totemic organization of the Hindus and the Untouchables has not yet been undertaken by students of anthropology. When such data is collected it would enable us to give a decisive opinion on the question raised in this Chapter. For the present, I am satisfied from such inquiries as I have made that the totems of the Untouchables of a particular village differ from the totems of the Hindus of the village.

Difference in totems between Hindus and Untouchables would be the best evidence in support of the thesis that the Untouchables are Broken Men belonging to a tribe different from the tribe comprising the village community. It may, however, be admitted that such direct evidence as has a bearing on the question remains to be collected. But facts have survived which serve as pointers and from which it can be said that the Untouchables were Broken men. There are two sets of such evidentiary facts.

One set of facts comprise the names *Antya*, *Antyaja* and *Antyavasin* given to certain communities by the Hindu Shastras. They have come down from very ancient past. Why were these names used to indicate a certain class of people? There seem to be some meaning behind these terms. The words are undoubtedly derivative. They are derived from the root *Anta.* What does the word *Anta* mean? Hindus learned in the Shastras argue that it means one who is born last and as the Untouchable according to the Hindu order of Divine creation is held to be born last, the word *Antya* means an Untouchable. The argument is absurd and does not accord with the Hindu theory of the order of creation. According to it, it is the Shudra who is born last. The Untouchable is outside the scheme of creation. The Shudra is *Savarna.* As against him the Untouchable is *Avarna, i.e.* outside the *Varna* system. The Hindu theory of priority in creation does not and cannot apply to the Untouchable. In my view, the word ***Antya*** means not end of creation but end of the village. It is a name given to those people who lived on the outskirts of the village. The word *Antya* has, therefore, a survival value. It tells us that there was a time when some people lived inside the village and some lived outside the village and that those who lived outside the village, *i.e.* on the *Antya* of the village, were called *Antyaja.*

Why did some people live on the border of the village? Can there be any other reason than that they were Broken Men who were aliens and who belonged to tribes different from those who lived inside the village? I cannot see any. That this is the real reason is to be found in the use of these particular words to designate them. The use of the words *Antya*, *Antyaja* and *Antyavasin* has thus double significance. In the first place, it shows that living in separate quarters was such a peculiar phenomenon that a new terminology had to be invented to give expression to it Secondly, the words chosen express in exact terms the conditions of the people to whom it applied namelv that they were aliens.

The second set of facts which shows that the Untouchables were Broken men relates to the position of a community called the Mahars. The Mahar community is a principle Untouchable community in Maharashtra. It is the single largest Untouchable community found in Maharashtra. The following facts showing the, relations between the Mahars and the Touchable Hindus are worthy of note: (1) The Mahars are to be found in every village; (2) Every village in Maharashtra has a wall and the Mahars have their quarters outside the wall; (3) The Mahars by turn do the duty of watch and ward on behalf of the village; and (4) The Mahars claim 52 rights against the Hindu villagers. Among these 52 rights the most important are :—

(i) The right to collect food from the villagers;

(ii) The right to collect corn from each villager at the harvest season ; and

(iii) The right to appropriate the dead animal belonging to the villagers.

The evidence arising from the position of the Mahars is of course confined to Maharastra. Whether similar cases are to be found in other parts of India has yet to be investigated. But if the Mahars case can be taken as typical of the Untouchables throughout India it will be accepted that there was a stage in the history of India when Broken Men belonging to other tribes came to the Settled tribes and made a bargain whereby the Broken men were allowed to settle on the border of the village, were required to do certain duties and in return were given certain rights. The Mahars have a tradition that the 52 rights claimed by them against the villagers were given to them by the Muslim kings of Bedar. This can only mean that these rights were very ancient and that the kings of Bedar only confirmed them.

These facts although meagre do furnish some evidence in support of the theory that the Untouchables lived outside the village from the very beginning. They were not deported and made to live outside the village *because* they were declared Untouchables. They lived outside the village from the beginning *because* they were Broken Men who belonged to a tribe different from the one to which the Settled tribe belonged.

The difficulty in accepting this explanation arises largely from the notion that the Untouchables were always Untouchables. This difficulty will vanish if it is borne in mind that there was a time when the ancestors of the present day Untouchables were not Untouchables *vis-a-vis* the villagers but were merely Broken Men, no more and no less, and the only difference between them and the villagers was that they belonged to different tribes.

CHAPTER V

Are There Parallel Cases ?

Are there any cases known to history of Broken Men living outside the village ? To this question it is possible to give an affirmative answer. Fortunately for us we have two reported cases which show that what is said to have occurred in India particularly has also actually occurred elsewhere. The countries wherein such a development has actually been reported to have taken place are Ireland and Wales.

The organization of the Irish village in primitive times can be seen from the Brehon Laws of Ireland. Some idea of it as revealed in these Laws may be obtained from the following summary given by Sir Henry Maine. Says Sir Henry Maine[1] :—

> "The Brehon Law discloses a stage when the tribe has long been settled, in all probability upon the tribal territory. It is of sufficient size and importance to constitute a political unit, and possibly at its apex is one of the numerous chieftain whom the Irish records call kings. The primary assumption is that the whole of the tribal territory belongs to the whole of the tribe, but in fact large portions of it have been permanently appropriated to minor bodies of tribesmen. A part is allotted in a special way to the chief as appurtenant to his office, and descends from chief to chief according to a special rule of succession. Other portions are occupied by fragments of the tribe, some of which are under minor chiefs while others, though not strictly ruled by a chief, have somebody of noble class to act as their representative. All the unappropriated tribelands are in a more special way the property of the tribe as a whole, and no portion can theoretically be subjected to more than a

1. Early History of Institutions, Lecture III, pp. 92-93.

temporary occupation. Such occupations are, however, frequent and among the holders of tribeland, on these terms, are groups of men calling themselves tribesmen, but being in reality associations formed by contract, chiefly for the purpose of pasturing cattle. Much of the common tribeland is not occupied at all, but constitutes, to use the English expression, the 'waste' of the tribe. Still this waste is constantly brought under tillage or permanent pasture by settlements of tribesmen, and upon it *cultivators and servile states are permitted to squat, particularly towards the border.* It is part of the territory over which the authority of the chief tends steadily to increase, and here it is that he settles his 'fuidhir' or stranger—tenants a *very important class—the outlaws and 'broken men' from other tribes who come to him for protection, and who are only connected with their new tribe by their dependence on its chief, and through the responsibility which he incurs for them*".

Who were the Fuidhirs? According to Sir Henry Maine the Fuidhirs were:

"Strangers or fugitives from other territories, men in fact, who had broken the original tribal bond which gave them a place in the community, and who had to obtain and then as best they might in a new tribe and new place. Society was violently disordered. The result was probably to fill the country with 'Broken Men' and such men could only find a home and protection by becoming Fuidhir tenants.

* * *

"The Fuidhir was not a tribesman but an alien. In all societies cemented together by kinship the position of the person who has lost or broken the bond of union is always extraordinarily miserable. He has not only lost his natural place in them but they have no room for him anywhere else".

II

Now as to Wales. The organization of the Welsh village in primitive times is described by Mr. Seebhom. According to Mr. Seebhom a village in Wales was a collection of homesteads. The homesteads were separated into two groups, the homesteads of the Free-tenants and the homesteads of the Unfree-tenants. Mr. Seebhom says that this separation in habitation was a common feature of the primitive village in Wales. Why were these Unfree-tenants made to live in a sepaate and detached placc? The oreason for this separation is explained by Mr. Seebhom in the following terms:—

> "At first sight there is a great confusion in the class of men mentioned in the ancient Welsh Laws—of tribesmen, *Uchelore bryre* and *innate boneddings*: of non-tribesmen, *talogo Aillte,Alltude*, etc. The confusion vanishes only when the principle underlying the constitution of tribal society is grasped. And this principle would apparently be a very simple one if could be freed from the complications of conquest and permanent settlement of land from the inroads of foreign law, custom, and nomenclature. To begin with there can be little doubt that the ruling principle underlying the structure of tribal society was that of blood relationship among the free tribesmen. No one who did not belong to a kindred could be a member of the tribe, which was in fact, a bundle of Welsh kindred. Broadly then under the Welsh tribal system there were two classes, those of Cymric blood—and those who were stranger in blood. There was a deep, if not unpassable, gulf between these two classes quite apart from any question of land or of conquest. It was a division in blood and it soon becomes apparent that the tenacity with which the distinction was maintained was at once one

1. The Tribal System in Wales. 2. Ibid. p. 9.
3. Ibid pp. 54-55.

of the strong distinctive marks of the tribal system and one of the main secrets of its strength."

III

This description of the organisation of the Irish and the Welsh villages in the primitive times leave no doubt that the case of the Untouchables of India is not the only case of a people living outside the village. It proves that in it was exhibited a universal phenomenon, and was marked by the following features:

1. That in primitive times the Village Settlement consisted of two parts. One part occupied by the community belonging to one tribe and another part occupied by the Broken Men of different tribes.
2. The part of the settlement occupied by the tribal community was regarded as the village proper. The Broken Men lived in the outskirts of the village,
3. The reason why the Broken Men lived outside the village was because they were aliens and did not belong to the tribal community.

The analogy between the Untouchables of India and the Fuidhirs of Ireland and the Alltudes of Wales is complete. The Untouchabls lived outside the village for the same reason for which the Fuidhirs and Alltudes had to live outside the village in Ireland and Wales. It is, therefore, clear that what is said about the Untouchable on the issue of their living outside the village is not without a parallel elsewhere.

CHAPTER VI

How Did Separate Settlements for Broken Men Disappear Elsewhere ?

That the Fuidhirs of Ireland and the Alltudes of Wales were Broken Men is true. That they lived in separate quarters is also a fact. But it is also true that the separate quarters of those Broken Men disappeared and they became part of the Settled tribe and were absorbed in it. This is somewhat strange. The Broken Men according to the theory set out before were given quarters outside the village because they belonged to a different tribe and, therefore, to different blood. How is it then that they were absorbed by the tribe later on? Why such a thing did not happen in India? These are questions which are natural and which call for an answer.

The question is integrally connected with the process of evolution through which Primitive Society came to be transferred into Modren Society. As has already been said this evolution has proceeded along two different lines. One marked the transformation of Primitive Society from Nomadic into a settled community. The other marked the transformation of Primitive Society from tribal into a territorial community. The question with which we are immediately concerned relates to the second line of evolution. For it is the substitution of common territory for common blood as the bond of union that is responsible for the disappearance of the separate quarters of the Broken Men. Why did Primitive Society substitute common territory for common blood as the bond of union? This is a question for which there is no adequate explanation. The origin of the change is very obscure. How the change was brought about is however quite clear.

At some stage there came into being in Primitive Society a rule whereby a non-tribesman could become a member of the tribe and become absorbed in it as a kindred. It was known as a rule of ennoblement. This rule was that if a non-tribesman lived next to the tribe or married within a tribe for a given number of generations he became their kindred.[1] Mr. Seebhom gives the following rules for a non-tribesman becoming a tribesman as it was found in the Welsh village system :

(1) Residence in Cymru (Wales) according to the tradition of South Wales made the descendant of a stranger at last, a Cymru, but not until continued to the ninth generation.

(2) Intermarriage with innate Cymraeses generation after generation made the descendent of a stranger an innate Cymru in the *fourth* generation. In other words, the original stranger's great-grandson, whose blood was at least seven-eighths Cymric was allowed to attain the right to claim the privileges of a tribesman.

Should not such a thing have happened in India ? It could have — indeed it should have. For a rule similar to that which existed in Ireland and Wales also existed in India. It is referred to by Manu. In Chaper X, verses 64-67, he says that a Shudra can be a Brahmin if he marries? for seven generations within the Brahmin Community. The ordinary rule of *Chaturvarna* was that a Shudra could never become a Brahmin. A Shudra was born and he did a Shudra and could not be made a Brahmin. But this rule of antiquity was so strong that Manu had to apply it to the Shudra. It is obvious that if this rule had continued to operate in India, the Broken Men of India would have been absorbed in the village community and their separate quarters would have ceased to exist.

Why did this not happen? The answer is that the notion of Untouchability supervened and perpetuated difference between kindred and non-kindred, tribesmen and non-tribesmen in another form; namely; between Touchables and Untouchables. It is this new factor which prevented the amalgamation taking place in the way in which it took place in Ireland and Wales, with the result that the system of separate quarters has become a perpetual and a permanent feature of the Indian village.

W. E. Hearn: The Aryan Household — Chapter VIII.

PART III

OLD THEORIES OF THE ORIGIN OF UNTOUCHABILITY

CHAPTER VII.

Racial Difference as the Origin of Untouchablity

What is the origin of Untouchability? As has been said the field is quite unexplored. No student of Sociology has paid any attention to it. Writers, other than Sociologists, who have written about India and her people have been content with merely recording the custom of Untouchability with varying degrees of disapprobation and leaving it at that. So far as my researches go, I have come across only one author who has attempted to explain how Untouchability has come about. It is Mr. Stanley Rice[1]. According to Mr. Rice—

> "*There is a strong probability that the outcasts were the survivors of the conquered peoples*, who, as caste tended to coincide with occupation, became the drum-beating, leather-working, and farm labouring classes to which as serfs they had been relegated from early times. *They were not the races* conquered by the Aryans; the *Paraiyans belonged to the aborigines who were conquered by the Dravidians* and being of a different race they were not admitted to the totem of similar clans with which marriage is always intimately connected, since that would have led to free intercourse and the gradual degradation of the race. But this prohibition cannot have been absolute; there are always exceptions. In the course of the centuries some forty or more the inevitable miscegenation may very well have obliterated the racial distinctions between aboriginal and early Dravidian. These people have been admitted to a sort of lowly participation in the Hindu system in the atmosphere of which they have lived for so long, for Hinduism is at once the most tolerant and intolarent of creeds. It does not proselytize; you cannot become a Hindu as you can become a

1. Hindu Customs And Their Origins : pp. 113-115. (Italics not in the original.)

Mussalman, and those within the fold are liable to the most rigid restrictions. But it has always been ready to embrace aboriginal tribes who are willing to submit to its laws, though it may assign to them a very lowly place and they have always been kept at a distance and have been excluded from the temples. It would seem, therefore, that anthropological arguments are in any case not conclusive when we consider these factors which must have profoundly modified the original racial characteristics and must have changed their outlook. *Thus the Dravidians applied to the Paraiyans the same test which the Aryans are assumed to have applied to the conquered inhabitants. They reduced them to the position of serfs and assigned to them 'those duties which it was thought beneath their own dignity to perform.* Nor was marriage the only consideration. The disabilities of the Paraiyans were due also—and to an even greater degree—to the mystical qualities inherent in Tabu. To admit such a man to the totem family was not only contrary to the social order; it would bring upon the clan the anger of their particular god. But to admit him to the worship of the god within the sacred precincts of a temple was to call down authentic fire from Heaven, whereby they would be consumed. It would be sacrilege of the same kind as the offering of unconsecrated or unorthodox fire by Korah, Dathan and Abhiram. But though debarred from taking an active part in worship, the Paraiyans might yet do the menial services connected with it, provided that they did not entail the pollution of the sacred building. In Chriistian terminology the Paraiyan, although he could neither officiate at the altar, nor preach a sermon nor even be one of the congregation, might still ring the bell—on one condition. He could not regard himself as of the communion; he was, in fact, ex-communicate. And as such, he was ceremonially unclean. No washing with water no cleansing ceremony, could remove that stain which was indelibly fixed by the operation of Tabu. To touch him, to have any dealings with him save as it were, at arm's length, was by a sort of contagious magic a defilement. You could employ him to till your field because that entailed no contact of any kind; beyond giving an order, you need have no further communication with him. The seal of pollution was set on his forehead; it was inherent in him as surely as the blood in his veins. And so from being the vile, degraded fellow which Indian opinion had made him, he became viler and more degraded from the kinds of occupation left open to him."

The theory of Mr. Rice really divides itself into parts. For, according to him, the origin of untoucha is to be found in two circumstances—Race and Oc tion. Obviously, they require separate consideration. Chapter will be devoted to an examination of his theo racial difference as the origin of untouchability.

The racial theory of Mr. Rice contains two eleme

(1) That the Untouchables are non-Aryan, Dravidian aboriginals; and

(2) That they were conquered and subjugated Dravidians.

This theory raises the whole question of the in of India by foreign invaders, the conquests made b and the social and cultural institutions that have re therefrom. According to Mr. Rice, there have bee invasions of India. First is the invasion of India by the dians. They conquered the non-Dravidian aborigin ancestors of the Untouchables, and made them Untouc The second invasion is the invasion of India by the The Aryans conquered the Dravidians. He does how the conquering Aryans treated the conquered dians. If pressed for an answer he might say they mad Shudras. So that we get a chain. The Dravidians i India and conquered the aborigines and made them U ables. After Dravidians came the Aryans. The conquered the Dravidians and made them Shudra theory is too mechanical, a mere speculation and to to explain a complicated set of facts relating to the origin of the Shudras and the Untouchables.

When students of ancient Indian history delve into the ancient past they do often come across four names, the Aryans, Dravidians, Dasas and Nagas. What do these names indicate ? This question has never been considered. Are these names Aryans, Dravidians, Dasas and Nagas the names of different races or are they merely different names for a people of the same race? The general assumption is that they are different races. It is an assumption on which theories like that of Mr. Rice, which seek to explain the social structure of the Hindu Society, particularly its class basis, are built. Before such a theory is accepted it is necessary to examine its foundations.

Starting with the Aryans it is beyond dispute that they were not a single homogeneous people. That they were divided into two[1] sections is beyond dispute. It is also beyond dispute that the two had different cultures. One of them may be called Rig Vedic Aryans and the other the Atharva Vedic Aryans. Their cultural cleavage appears to be complete. The Rig Vedic Aryans believed in Yajna. The Atharva Vedic Aryans believed the Magis. Their mythologies were different. The Rig Vedic Aryans believed in the Deluge and the creation of their race from Manu. The Atharva Vedic Aryans did not believe in Deluge but believed in the creation of their race from Brahma or Prajapati. Their literary developments also lay along different paths. The Rig Vedic Aryans produced Brahmans, Sutras and Aranyakas. The Atharva Vedic Aryans produced the Upanishads. Their cultural conflict was so great that the Rig Vedic Aryans would not for a long time admit the sanctity of the Atharva Veda nor of the Upanishads and when they did recognize it they called it Vedanta which contrary to the current meaning of the word—namely, essence of the Vedas—originally meant something outside the boundary of the Vedas and, therefore, not so sacred as the Vedas and regarded its study as Anuloma. Whether these two sections of Aryans were two different races we do not know. We do not know

1. For an exhaustive treatment of the subject see my book "Who Were the Shudras?".

whether the word Aryan is a term indicative of race. Historians have therefore made a mistake in proceeding on the assumption that the Aryans were a separate race.

A greater mistake lies in differentiating the Dasas from the Nagas. The Dasas are the same as Nagas. Dasas is merely another name for Nagas. It is not difficult to understand how the Nagas came to be called Dasas in the Vedic literature. Dasa is a Sanskritized form of the Indo-Iranian word Dahaka. Dahaka was the name of the king of the Nagas.[1] Consequently, the Aryans called the Nagas after the name of their king Dahaka, which in its Sanskrit form became Dasa a generic name applied to all the Nagas.

Who were the Nagas? Undoubtedly they were non-Aryans. A careful study of the Vedic literature[2] reveals a spirit of conflict, of a dualism, and a race for superiority between two distinct types of culture and thought. In the Rig Veda, we are first introduced to the Snake-god in the form of Ahi Vitra, the enemy of the Aryan god Indra. Naga, the name under which the Snake-god was to become so famous in later days, does not appear in early Vedic literature. Even when it does for the first time in the Satapatha Brahmana (XI. 2,7,12), it is not clear whether a great snake or a great elephant is meant. But this does not conceal the nature of Ahi Vitra, since he is described always in Rig Veda as the serpant who lay around or hidden in waters, and as holding a full control, over the waters of heaven and earth alike.

It is also evident from the hymns that refer to Ahi Vitra, that he received no worship from the Aryan tribes and was only regarded as an evil spirit of considerable power who must be fought down.

The mention of the Nagas in the Rig Veda shows that the Nagas were a very ancient people. It must also be remembered that the Nagas were in no way an aboriginal or uncivilized people. History shows a very close association by intermarriage between the Naga people with the Royal

1. On this point see my Volume : "Who Were the Shudras ?"

2. For the facts stated in the next few pages, see a Paper on the Nagas and the Naga cult in Ancient Indian History by Miss Karunakara Gupta in the Proceedings of the Third Session of the Indian History Congress (1939)p,. 214 onwards,

families of India. The Devagiri record of the Kadamba king Krisnavarmma[1] connects the beginning of the Kadamba-kula with the Nagas. The Royakota[2] grant of 9th century A.D. mentions the marriage of Asvathama with a Nagi and the foundation of the Pallava line by Skandasishya, the issue of this marriage. Virakurcha, who according to another Pallava inscription dated in the 9th century A.D. was the ruler of the dynasty, is also mentioned in the same inscription as having married a Nagi and 'obtained from her the insignia of royalty.'[3] The marriage of Gautamiputra, the son of the Vakataka king Pravarasena, with the daughter of the Bharasiva king Bhava Naga, is a historical fact. So is the marriage of Chandragupta II with princess Kuvera Naga 'of Naga Kula'.[4] A Tamil poet asserts that Kokkilli, an early Chola king, had married a Naga princess.[5] Rajendra Chola is also credited to have won 'by his radiant beauty the hand of the noble daughter of Naga race[6]. The Navasahasanka Charita describes the marriage of the Paramara king Sindhuraja (who seems to have reigned towards the early part of the 10th Century A.D.) with the Naga princess Sasiprabha, with such exhaustive details in so matter-of-fact-a-manner as to make us almost feel certain that there must have been some historical basis for this assertion.[7] From the Hạrsha inscription of V.S. 1030-973 A.D. we know that Guvaka I, who was the sixth king in the genealogy upwards from Vigraharaja Chahamana and thus might be supposed to have been ruling towards the middle of the 9th Century was "famous as a hero in the assemblies of the Nagas and other princes."[8] Sanatikara of the Bhaumn dynasty of Orissa, one of whose dates was most probably 921 A.D., is mentioned in an inscription of his son as having married Tribhuana Mahadevi of the Naga family.[9]

Not only did the Naga people occupy a high cultural level but history shows that they ruled a good part of India.

1. I.A. VII. p. 34
2. E.I. XV. p. 246
3. S.I.I. II. p. 508
4. E.I.XV. p. 41
5. E.I. XV. p. 249
6. I.A.XXII. pp. 144-149
7. E.I. I. p. 229
8. E.I. II. p. 117
9. J.B.O.R.S. XVI. p. 771

That Maharashtra is the home of the Nagas goes without saying. Its people and its kings were Nagas.[1]

That Andhradesa and its neighbourhood were under the Nagas during the early centuries of the Christian era is suggested by evidence from more sources than one, The Satavahanas, and their successors, the Chutu Kula Satakarnis drew their blood more or less from the Naga stock. As Dr. H. C. Roy Chaudhri has pointed out, the Dvatrimasatpu-kalitta represents Salivaharana, the mythological representative of the Satavahana dynasty, as cf mixed Brahmana and the Naga origin.[2] This is amply attested to by the typical Naga names which occur in their dynastic lists. That the Nagas grew to be very powerful towards the end of the Satavahana rule is also proved by a number of facts. A chief called Skandanaga is found ruling the Bellary district, in the reign of Pulumavi, the last king of the màin Satavahana line. Secondly. Naga Mulanika the daughter of a Chutu king, is mentioned as making a gift of a Naga, together with her son, who is called Sivakanda-Naga-Sri. All the known kings of this line bear the same name and thus prove a close association with the Nagas. Thirdly, the name of Uragapura, the capital of Soringoi, suggest not an isolated reign of one Naga king but a Naga Settlement in that locality of tolerably long duration.

From Buddhist tradition of Ceylon and Siam we also know that there was a Naga country called Majerika near the Diamond Sands, i.e. Karachi.[3]

Then during the third and early part of the 4th Century A.D. Northern India also was ruled by a number of Naga kings is clearly proved by Furanic as well as numismaric and epigraphic evidence. Three independent groups of Vidisa, Campavati or Padmavati and Mathura are distinctly mentioned in such a way as to leave little doubt of their importance. The name Bhava Naga, the only known king of the Bharasiva dynasty, also seems to connect him with the Nagas. It is not possible to enter here into a discussion of the coins of the second group, or the question of indentification of

1. Rajwade.

2. I. P. H. A. I, p. 280.

3. Cunningham A. Geo. India, pp. 611-12.

Achyuta Ganapati Naga or Nagasena of Allahabad Pillar inscription with these Puranic Naga kings.[1] Of all the Nagas referred to in ancient Indian History, the North Indian Naga houses of the 4th century A.D. stand out as the most prominent and historically the most tangible. We do not know whether Nagabhatta and his son Maharaja Mohesvara Naga of the Lahore Copper Seal[3] belonged to any of these three groups or formed a separate Naga family by themselves. But all this sufficiently justifies the conclusion of Dr. C.C. Roy Chaudhri that the Kushana kingdom of Northern India disappeared in the 4th Century A.D. having been conquered by the Nagas. These Nagas must have been ruling over different portions of Uttarapatha till they were themselves swept away before the conquering arms of Somudrguprta.

As late as the time of Skandagupta, however, we find one Sarvanaga as the governor of Antarvedi.[4] In the neighbourhood of Surashtra and Bharukaccha especially, the Nagas seem to have held a prominent position down to the 6th Century A.D. From the Junagadh inscription Skandagupta appears to have dealt severely with a Naga rebellion.[5] In 570 A.D. Dadda I Gurjara uproofed the Nagas.[6] who have been indentifled with the jungle tribles ruled over by Brihul laka or Broach.[7] Dhruvasena II's grant of G.S. 334 (645 A D.) also mentions as Dutaka the Pramatri Srinaga.[8]

The next important revival of the Nagas particularly in Central India seems to date about the 9th Century A,D. In 800 A.D. Maharaja Tivaradeva of Sripura in Kosala most probably defeated a Naga tribe.[9] Sometime after this period, we also note two references to Nagas in the inscription of Bengal. The Ramganj record of Mahamandalika Isvara Ghosha introduces us to a Ghosha Naga family of Dhekkari, which was to be assigned to 11th century[10] A.D. The

1. C. M. I. pp. 23-24
2. P. H. A. I. p. 364
3. G. I. p. 284
4. G. I. p. 68
5. G. I. p. 59
6. I. A. XIII pp. 82
7. B. Gaz. I.i. 115
8. E. I. I. p. 92
9. G. I. p. 298
10 Bhandarkar's List No. 2100.

Bhuvanesvara Prasasti of Bhatta Bhavadeva, the minister of Harivarmadeva in 12th century[1] A.D also refers to destruction of Naga kings by him. The Ramacharita mentions the conquest of Utkala, the kingdom of Bhava-Bhushana-Santati, by Ramapala, but it is not clear whether in this case the Nagas or the Chandras were meant. The greater probability would however lie in favour of the former, since they were the more well known.

It was in the period 10th-12th Century A.D. that the different branches of the Sendraka, Sinda, or Chindaka family, which called themselves lords of Bhogavati and Naga-vamsi gradually spread themselves over different portions of Central India, particularly Baster. The Nagattaras of Begur, too, appear in an inscription of the 10th Century[2] A.D. as having fought against king Viramahendra, on behalf of the W. Ganga king Ereyappa and being distinguished for bravery in the fight. If the evidence of Navasahasanka Charita is accepted, then the Naga king, whose daughter Sasiprabha was married to Sindhuraja Paramara, must also have been ruling in Ratnavati on the Narmada at about this period.

Who are the Dravidians? Are they different from the Nagas? Or are they two different names for a people of the same race? The popular view is that the Dravidians and Nagas are names of two different races. This statement is bound to shock many people. Nonetheless, it is a fact that the term Dravidians and Nagas are merely two different names for the same people.

It is not to be denied that very few will be prepared to admit the proposition that the Dravidians and Nagas are merely two different names for the same people and fewer that the Dravidians as Nagas occupied not merely South India but that they occupied the whole of India—South as well as North. Nonetheless, these are historical truths.

Let us see what the authorities have to say on the subject. This is what Mr. Dikshitiar, a well-known South Indian scholar, has to say on the subject in his[3] Paper on *South India in the Ramayana*:

1. Inscription of Bengal III pp. 30 ff.
2. E.I. VI. p. 45

> "The Nagas, another tribe—semi-divine in character, with their tolein as serpent, spread throughout India, from Taksasila in the North-West to Assam in the North-East and to Ceylon and South India in the South. At one time they must have been powerful. Contemporaneous with the Yakwas or perhaps subsequent to their fall as a political entity, the Nagas rose to prominence in South India. Not only parts of Ceylon but ancient Malabar were the territories occupied by the ancient Nagas . . . In the Tamil classics of the early centuries after Christ, we hear frequent references to Naganadu . . . Remnants of Naga worship are still lingering in Malabar, and the temple in Nagercoil in South Travancore is dedicated to Naga worship even today. All that can be said about them is that they were a sea-faring tribe. Their womenfolk were renowned for their beauty. Apparently the Nagas had become merged with the Cheras who rose to power and prominence at the commencement of the Christian Era."

Further light is thrown on the subject by C. F. Oldham who has made a deep study of it. According to Mr. Oldham:[2]

> "The Dravidian people have been divided, from ancient times, into Cheras, Cholas and Pandyas.
>
> Chera, or Sera (in old Tamil Sarai) is the Dravidian equivalent for Naga; Cheramandala, Nagadwipa, or the Naga country. This seems to point distinctly to the Asura origin of the Dravidians of the South. But in addition to this there still exists, widely spread over the Ganges valley, a people who call themselves Cherus or Seoris, and who claim descent from the serpent-gods.[3] The Cherus are of very ancient race;

1. Proceedings of the Seventh All-India Oriental Conference, pp. 248-49
2. The Sun and the Serpent, pp. 157-161
3. Elliot Sup. Glossary N. W. F., 135, 136

they are believed to have once held a great portion of the valley of the Ganges, which, as we have already seen, was occupied in very early times by Naga tribes. The Cherus appear to have been gradually ousted from their lands, during the troublous times of the Mohammedan invasions, and they are now poor and almost landless. There can be little doubt that these people are kinsmen of the Dravidian Cheras.

The Cherus have several peculiar customs and amongst them one which seems to connect them with the Lichavis, as well as with the Newars of Nepal. This is the election of a raja for every five or six houses, and his investiture, in due form, with the tilak or royal frontal mark.[1] Both Lichavis and Newars had many customs in common with the Dravidians of the South. Each venerated the serpent, Karkotaka Naga being to Nepal what Nila Naga was to Kashmir. A Naga, too, was the tutelary deity of Vaisali, the Lichavi capital. The marital relations of Newars and Lichavis closely resembled those of the Tamil people, and go far to show a common origin.

Property amongst the Newars descended in the female line, as it once did amongst the Arattas, Bahikas or Takhas of the Punjab, whose sisters' sons, and not their own, were their heirs.[2] This is still a Dravidian custom. In short, a recent Dravidian writer, Mr. Balakrishna Nair, says that his people 'appear to be, in nearly every particular, the kinsfolk of the Newars.'[3]

Besides all this, however, there are other links connecting the Naga people of the South with those of the north of India. In an inscription discovered by Colonel Tod at Kanswah near the river Chambal, a Raja, called Salindra, 'of the race of Sarya, a tribe renowned amongst the

1. Sherring Races of N.W.P., 376,377
2. Mahabharatta, Karna, p. xiv
3. Calcutta Review, July, 1896.

tribes of the mighty' is said to be ruler of Takhya.[1]

This was evidently the Takhya or Takha kingdom of the Punjab, which was visited by Hiouen Tsiang,[2] and which has been already referred to. It seems, therefore, that the Naga people of Takhya were known also by the name of Sarya.

Again, in the outer Himalaya, between the Sutlej and Beas Valleys, is a tract of country called Saraj, or Seoraj. In this district the Naga demigods are the chief deities worshipped.

There is another Seoraj in the Upper Chinab Valley, and this too is occupied by a Naga-worshipping people.

The name Saraj, or Seoraj, appears to be the same as the Sarya of Colonel Tod's inscription and as Seori, which is the alternative name of the Cherus of the Ganges Valley. It also seems to be identical with Sarai, which we have already seen, is the old Tamil name for the Chera or Naga. Apparently, therefore, the Saryas or Takhya, the Saraj people of the Sutlej Valley, the Seoris or Cherus of the valley of the Ganges, and the Cheras, Seras, or Keralas of Southern India, are but different branches of the same Naga-worshipping people.

It may be noted, too, that in some of the Himalayan dialects, Kira or Kiri means a serpent. This name, from which was perhaps derived the term Kirate so often applied to the people of the Himalayas, is found in the Rajatarangini, where it is applied to a people in or near Kashmir. The Kiras are mentioned by Varaha Mihira, and in a copper plate published by Prof. Kielhorn.[3]

An inscription at the Baijnath temple in the

1. Annals of Rajasthan, i.795
2. Hiouen Tsiang, Beal, i.165
3. Rajatarangini, Stein, viii. 27, 67
   Rapson J.R.A.S., July 1900, 533

Kangra valley gives Kiragrams as the then name of the place.[1] This, in the local dialect, would mean the village of serpents. The Naga is still a popular deity at Baijnath, and throughout the neighbouring country. The term Kira is thus an equivalent for Naga, and it can scarcely be doubted that the serpent-worshipping Kiras of the Himalayas were closely related to the Dravidian Keras, Cheras or Keralas of the South.

Similarity of name is not always to be trusted, but here we have something more. These people, whose designation is thus apparently the same, are all of Solar race; they all venerate the hooded serpent; and they all worship, as ancestors, the Naga demi-gods.

From the foregoing it would seem tolerably certain that the Dravidians of Southern India were of the same stock as the Nagas or Asuras of the North."

It is thus clear that the Nagas and Dravidians are one and the same people. Even with this much of proof, people may not be found ready to accept the thesis. The chief difficulty in the way of accepting it lies in the designation of the people of South India by the name Dravidian. It is natural for them to ask why the term Dravidian has come to be restricted to the people of South India if they are really Nagas. Critics are bound to ask: If the Dravidians and the Nagas are the same people, why is the name Nagas not used to designate people of South India also. This is no doubt a puzzle. But it is a puzzle which is not beyond solution. It can be solved if certain facts are borne in mind.

The first thing to be borne in mind is the situation regarding language. Today the language of the Southern India differs from that of the people of Northern India. Was this always so? On this question the observations of Mr. Oldham[2] are worth attention.

"It is evident that the old Sanskrit grammarians considered the language of the Dravidian

J.R.A.S., Jan. 1903, p. 37

The Sun and the Serpent prefer to author.

countries to be connected with the vernaculars of northern India; and that, in their opinion, it was especially related to the speech of those people who, as we have seen, were apparently descendants of the Asura tribes. Thus, in the 'Shahasha Chandrika', Lakshmidhara says that the Paisachi language is spoken in the Paisachi countries of Pandya, Kekaya, Vahlika, Sahya, Nepala, Kuntala, Sudesha, Bhota, Gandhara, Haiva and Kanojana: and that these are the Paisachi countries.[1] Of all the vernacular dialects, the paisachi is said to have contained the smallest infusion of Sanskrit.[2]

That the Asuras originally spoke a language which differed from that of the Aryas seems evident. Several passages are quoted by Prof. Muir, from the Rig Veda, in which the word 'mridavach' is applied to the speech of the Asuras (R.vi.74,2; v.vi.3; v.vii.6). Of these passages, Professor Muir observes: 'The word mridavach, which I have translated "injuriously speaking", is explained by Sayana as meaning "one whose organs of speech are destroyed",[3] The original meaning of the expression was, doubtless that the language of the Asuras was more or less unintelligible to the Aryas. The same explanation will apply to another passage in the Rig Veda, where it is said: 'May we (by propitiating Indra) conquer the ill-speaking man.'[4]

From the Satapatha Brahmana we find that 'the Asuras, being deprived of speech, were undone, crying, 'He lava', 'He lava'. Such was the unintelligible speech which they uttered. And he who speaks thus is a Mlecha. Hence, let no Brahman speak barbarous language, since such is the speech of Asuras.[5]

1 and 2. Muir O.S.T. ii. 49

3. Muir O.S.T.ii. 49

4. Rig Veda Wilson VII, xviii. 13

5. Satapatha Br. iii. 2,1,23

We learn from Manu, that 'those tribes who are outside of the classes produced from the mouth, arms, thighs and feet of Brahman, whether they speak the language of the Mlechas or of the Aryas, are called Dasyus.'[1] In the time of Manu, therefore, the Aryan language and that of the Mlechas or Asuras were both in use. At the period described in the Mahabharata, however, the Asura language must have almost died out amongst the Aryanized tribes; as Vidura addressed Yudishthra in the Mlecha tongue, so as to be unintelligible to all except Yudishthra.[2]

At a later period than this, however, the grammarian Rama Tarkavagisa refers to 'those who speak like Nagas.'[3] It would seem, therefore, that the unregenerate Asuras retained the language, as well as the religion and customs, of their forefathers long after their converted brethren had discarded them. It was evidently amongst these unregenerate tribes that the Paisachi dialects were in use; and amongst these tribes, as we have just seen, were the Dravidian Pandyas.[4]

This view, that the Tamil and cognate tongues were founded upon the ancient Asura speech, is very strongly confirmed by the fact that the language of the Brahuis, a tribe on the borders of Sind, has been found to be very closely allied to them. Indeed, Dr. Caldwell says: 'The Brahui (language) enables us to trace the Dravidian race, beyond the Indus, to the southern confines of Central Asia.[5] This country, as I have already pointed out, was the home of the Asuras or Nagas, to which race apparently belonged the founders of the Dravidian kingdoms.

1. Manu, Haughton x. 45
2. Mahabharata Adi, Jatagriha, p. cxlvii.
3. Muir, O.S.T., ii. 52
4. Ibid. 49
5. Grammar of Drav. Lang., Intro., 44

> Taking into consideration all the evidence which has been brought forward, the only possible conclusion seems to be, that the Dravidians, of the south of India, were of the same stock as the Asuras or Nagas of the North."

The second thing to be borne in mind is that the word 'Dravida' is not an original word. It is the Sanskritized form of the word 'Tamil'. The original word 'Tamil' when imported into Sanskrit became *Damila*[1] and later on *Damilla* became Dravida. The word Dravida is the name of the language of the people and does not denote the race of the people. The third thing to remember is that Tamil or Dravida was not merely the language of South India but before the Aryans came it was the language of the whole of India,[2] and was spoken from Kashmere to Cape Camorin. In fact, it was the language of the Nagas throughout India. The next thing to note is the contact between the Aryan and the Nagas and the effect it produced on the Nagas and their language. Strange as it may appear the effect of this contact on the Nagas of North India was quite different from the effect it produced on the Nagas of South India. The Nagas in North India gave up Tamil which was their mother tongue and adopted Sanskrit in its place. The Nagas in South India retained Tamil as their mother tongue and did not adopt Sanskrit the language of the Aryans. If this difference is borne in mind it will help to explain why the name Dravida came to be applied only for the people of South India. The necessity for the application of the name Dravida to the Nagas of Northern India had ceased because they had ceased to speak the Dravida language. But so far as the Nagas of South India are concerned not only the propriety of calling them Dravida had remained in view of their adherence to the Dravida language but the necessity of calling them Dravida had become very urgent in view of their being the only people speaking the Dravida language after the Nagas of the North had ceased to use it. This is the real reason why the people of South India have come to be called Dravidians.

The special application of the use of the word Dravida

1. B.R. Bhandarkar, Lectures on the Ancient History of India (1919), p. 30
2. Ibid pp., 25-28.

for the people of South India must not, therefore, obscure the fact that the Nagas and Dravidas are the one and the same people. They are only two different names for the same people. Nagas was a racial or cultural name and Dravida was their linguistic name.

Thus the Dasas are the same as the Nagas and the Nagas are the same as the Dravidians. In other words what we can say about the races of India is that there have been at the most only two races in the field, the Aryans and the Nagas. Obviously the theory of Mr. Rice must fall to the ground. For it postulates three races in action when as a matter of fact

II

Granting however that there was a third aboriginal race living in India before the advent of the Dravidians, can it be said that these pre-Dravidian aboriginals were the ancestors of the present day Untouchables of India? There are two tests we can apply to find the truth. One is the anthropometric test and the other is the ethnological.

Considered in the light of the anthropometric characteristics of the Indian people Prof. Ghurey has something very striking to say in his volume on 'Caste and Race in India' from which the following is an extract :

> "Taking the Brahmin of the United Provinces as the typical representative of the ancient Aryans we shall start comparisons with him. If we turn to the table of differential indices we find that he shows a smaller differential index as compared with the Chuhra and the Khatri of the Punjab than with any caste from the United Provinces except the Chhatri. The differential index between the Khatri and the Chuhra[1] is the only slightly less than that between the Brahmin of the United Provinces and the Chuhraof the punjab. This means that the Brahmin of the United Provinces has closer physical affinities with the Chuhra and the

1. Chuhra is an Untouchable of the Punjab.

Khatri of the Punjab than with any caste from his own province except the very high caste of the Chhatri. .. The reality of this close affinity between the United Provinces Brahmin and the Punjab Chuhra is more clearly brought out if we look at the table of differential indices between the United Provinces Brahmin and the Brahmins of other regions. Even the differential index between the United Provinces Brahmin and the Bihar Brahmins, who from what we know about the history of spread of the Aryan culture, is expected to be very nearly allied to the former, is just as high as that between the United Provinces Brahmin and the Chuhra. .. On historical ground we expect Bihar to approximate to the United Provinces. On referring to the table we find that the Kurmi comes near to the Brahmin, and the Chamar and the Dom[1] stand much differentiated from him. But the Chamar in this case is not as much distinct from the Brahmin as the United Provinces Chamar is from the United Provinces Brahmin. The table for Bengal shows that the Chandal[2] who stands sixth in the scheme of a social precedence and whose touch pollutes, is not much differentiated from the Brahmin, from whom the Kayasthas, second in rank, can hardly be said to be distinguished. In Bombay the Deshastha Brahmin bears as closer affinity to the Son-Koli, a fisherman caste, as to his own compeer, the Chitpavan Brahmin. The Mahar, the Untouchable of the Maratha region, come next together with the Kubi, the peasont. Then follow in order the Shenvi Brahmin, the Negar Brahmin and the high caste Maratha. These results are rather old. Stated in a generalized form they mean that there is no correspondence between social gradation and physical differentiation in Bombay.

1. Dom is an Untouchable of Bihar.
2. Chandal is an Untouchable of Bengal.

Finally we come to Madras. Here we must treat the different linguistic areas separately for the schemes of social precedence in the various areas are different. According to the average given by Risely and by E. Thurston the order of castes is as follows :

Kapu, Sale, Malla, Golla, Madiga, Fogata and Komati.

According to their social status they are ranked as below :

Brahmin, Komati, Golla, Kapu and others and Sale, Fagota and others.

Mala Madiga occupy the lowest rank being the Pariahs of the Telugu country. In the Canarese the nasal index gives the following order :

Karnatak Smarts, Brahmin, Bant, Billiva, Mandya Brahmin, Vakkaliga, Ganiga, Linga Banajiga, Panchala Kurha, Holeya, Deshastha Brahmin, Toreya and Bedar.

In the scheme of social precedence the castes are as under :

Brahmin, Bant and Vakkaliga, Toreya, etc., Kuruba and Ganiga Badaga and Krumba and Solaga, Billiva, Beda Holeya.

The significance of the comparison is enhanced when we remember that the nasal index of the Holeya, the Untouchables of the Canarese region is 75·1 that of the highest of the Brahmin being 71·5 while those of the jungle Krumba and the Solaga, who when Hinduised occupy the rank allotted to them in the list, are 86.1 and 85·1 respectively.

The Tamil castes may be arranged according to their nasal index as follows :-

Ambattan, Vellai, Ediayan, Agamudaiyan, Tamil Brahmin, Palli, Malaiyali, Shanan and Parayan. The Nasal indices of four typical Malaylam castes are: Tiyan, 75; Nambudir 75·5; Nayar 76·7; |Charuman 77·2. The order of social precedence among these is: Nambudri, Nayar, Tiyan and Charuman. The nasal index of the Kanikar, a jungle tribe of Travancore is 8'46. Thus, the Charuman (an Unapproachable) belonging to the same race as the Brahmin rather than to Kanikar."

To omit from the above extract what is said about other communities and to draw attention to what relates to the Untouchables only, it is clear that the nasal index of the Chuhra (the Untouchables) of the Punjab is the same as the nasal index of the Brahmin of the United Provinces; the nasal index of the Chamar (the Untouchables) or Bihar is not very much distinct from the Brahmin of Bihar; the nasal index of the Holeya (an Untouchable) of the Canarese is far higher than that of the Brahmin of Karnatak and that the nasal index of the Cheruman (an Unapproachable lower than the Pariah) of the Tamil belongs to the same race as the Brahmin of the Tamil Nad. If anthropometry is a science which can be depended upon to determine the race of a people, then the result obtained by the application of anthropometry to the various strata of Hindu society disprove that the Untouchables belong to a race different from the Aryans and the Dravidians. The measurements establish that the Brahmin and the Untouchables belong to the same race. From this it follows that if the Brahmins are Aryans the Untouchables are also Aryans. If the Brahmins are Dravidians the Untouchables are also Dravidians. If the Brahmins are Nagas, the Untouchables are also Nagas. Such being the facts, the theory propounded by Mr. Rice must be said to be based on a false foundation.

III

The racial theory of Untouchability not only runs counter to the results of anthropometry, but it also finds very little. support from such facts as we know about the ethnology of India That the people of India were once organized on tribal basis is quite well known, and although the tribes have become casites the tribal organization still remains intact. Each trrbe was divided into clans and the clans were composed of woups of families. Each group of families had a totem which gas some object animate or inanimate. Those who had a common totem formed an exagomous group popularly known as Gotra or Kula. Families having a common gotra were not allowed to intermarry for they were supposed to be descended from the same ancestor having the same blood running in their veins. Having regard to this fact an examination of the distribution of the totems among the different castes and communties should serve as good a test for determining race as anthropometry has been.

Unfortunately, the study of the totems and their distribution among different communities has been completely neglected by students of sociology. This neglect is largely due to the current view propagated by the Census Commissioners that the real unit of the Hindu social system and the basis of the fabric of Hindu society is the sub-caste founded on the rule of endogamy. Nothing can be a greater mistake than this. The unit of Hindu society is not the sub-caste but the family founded on the rule of exogamy. In this sense the Hindu family is fundamentally a tribal organization and not a social organization as the sub-caste is. The Hindu family is primarily guided in the matter of marriage by consideration of *Kul* and *Gotra* and only secondarily by considerations of caste and sub-caste. *Kul* and *Gotra* are Hindu equivalents of the totem of the Primitive Society. This shows that the Hindu society is still tribal in its organization with the family at its base observing the rules of exogamy based on *Kul* and *Gotra*. Castes and sub-castes are social organizations which are superimposed over the tribal organization and the rule of endogamy enjoined by them does not do away with the rule of exogamy enjoined by the tribal organizations of *Kul* and *Gotra*.

The importance of recognizing the fact that it is the family which is fundamental and not the sub-caste is obvious. It would lead to the study of the names of *Kul* and *Gotra* prevalent among Hindu families. Such a study would be a great help in determining the racial composition of the people of India. If the same *Kul* and *Gotra* were found to exist in different castes and communities it would be possible to say that the castes though socially different were racially one. Two such studies have been made, one in Maharashtra by Risley[1] and another in the Punjab,[2] by hu Rose and the

1. Census of India 1901. Ethnographical Appendices.
2. Glossary of Tribes and Castes in the Punjab by Rose, Vol, III, p.76.

result flatly contradict the theory that the Untouchables are racially different from the Aryans or the Dravidians. The main bulk of the population in Maharastra consists of Marathas. The Mahars are the Untouchables of Maharastra. The anthropological investigation shows that both have the same *Kul*. Indeed the identity is so great that there is hardly a *Kul* among the Marathas which is not to be found among the Mahars and there is no *Kul* among the Mahars which is not to be found among the Marathas. Similarly, in the Punjab one main stock of people consists of Jats. The Mazabi Sikhs are Untouchables most of them being Chamars by caste. Anthropological investigation shows that the two have the same *Gotras*. Given these facts how can it be argued that the Untouchables belong to a different race? As I have said if totem, kul, and gotra, have any significance it means that those who have the same totem must have been kindred. If they were kindred they could not be persons of different race.

The racial theory of the origin of Untouchability must, therefore, be abandoned.

CHAPTER VIII

Occupational origin of Untouchability

We may now turn to the occupational theory of the origin of Untouchability. According to Mr. Rice the origin of Untouchability is to be found in the unclean and filthy occupations of the Untouchables. The theory is a very plausible one. But there are certain difficulties in the way of its being accepted as a true explanation of the origin of Untouchability. The filthy and unclean occupations which the Untouchables perform are common to all human societies. In every human Society there are people who perform these occupations. Why were such people not treated as Untouchables in other parts of the world ? The second question is: Did the Dravidians have a nausea against such callings or against persons engaged in them ? On this point, there is no evidence. But we have evidence about the Aryans. That evidence shows that the Aryans were like other people and their notions of purity and impurity did not fundamentally differ from those of other ancient people. One has only to consider the following texts from Narada Smriti to show that the Aryans did not at all mind engaging themselves in filthy occupations. In Chapter V Narada is dealing with the subject matter of breach of contract of service. In this Chapter, there occur the following verses

1. The sages have distinguished five sorts of attendants according to law. Among these are four sorts of labourers; the slaves (are the fifth category of which there are) fifteen species.
2. A student, an apprentice, a hired servant, and fourthly an official.
3. The sages have declared that the state of dependence is common to all these but that their respective position and income depends on their particular caste and occupations.
4. Know that there are two sorts of occupations ; pure work and impure work; *impure work is that*

done by the slaves. Pure work is that done by labourers.

5. *Sweeping the gateway, the privy, the road and the place for rubbish; shampooing the secret parts of the body; gathering and putting away the leaving of food, ordure and urine.*

6. *And lastly, rubbing the master's limbs when desired; this should be regarded as impure work. All other work besides this is pure.*

25. Thus have the four classes of servants doing pure work been enumerated. All the others who do dirty work are slaves, of whom there are fifteen kinds:[1]

It is clear that impure work was done by the slaves and that the impure work included scavenging. The question that arises is: Who were these slaves? Were they Aryans or non-Aryans? That slavery existed among the Aryans admits of no doubt. An Aryan could be a slave of an Aryan. No matter to what Varna an Aryan belonged he could be a slave. A Kshatriya could be a slave. So could a Vaishya. Even a Brahmin was not immune from the law of slavery. It is when *Chaturvarna* came to be recognized as a law of the land that a change was made in the system of slavery. What this change was can be seen from the following extract from the Narada Smriti :

"39. In the inverse order of the (four) castes slavery is not ordained, except where a man violated

The fifteen classes of slaves are defiued by the Narada Smiriti in the following verses :

V. 26. One born at (his master's) house; one purchased one received (by gift); one obtained bv inheritance; one maintained during a general famine; one pledged by his rightful owner.

V. 27. One released from heavy debt; one made captive in fight; one won through a wager; one who has come forward declaring 'I am thine.' An apostate from asceticism; one enslaved for a stipulated period.

V. 28. One who has become slave in order to get a maintenance; one enslaved on account of his connection with a female slave; and one self-sold. These are 15 classes of slaves as declared by law.

> the duties peculiar to his caste. Slavery (in that respect) is analogous to the condition of a wife."

Yajnavalkya also says that :

> "183(2) Slavery is in the descending order of the *Varnas* and not in the ascending order."

This is explained by Vijnaneswara in his Mitakshara, a Commentary on Yajnavalkya Smriti. in the following terms:—

> "Of the Varna such as the Brahmin and the rest, a state of slavery shall exist in the descending order (Anulomeyna). Thus, of a Brahmin, a Kshatriya and the rest may become a slave; of a Kshatriya, the Vaishya and the Shudra; and of a Vaishya, a Shudra; this state of slavery shall operate in the descending order."

The change was a mere reorganization of slavery and the basis of the principles of graded inequality which is the soul of Chaturvarna. To put it in a concrete form, the new law declared that a Brahmin could have a Brahmin, Kshatriya, Vaishya and a Shudra as his slave. A Kshatriya could have a Kshatriya, a Vaishya and a Shudra as his slave. A Vaishya could have a Vaishya and a Shudra as his slave. A Shudra could have a Shudra only. With all this, the law of slavery remained and all Aryans whether they were Brahmins, Kshatriyas, Vaishyas or Shudras if they become slaves were subject to it.

Having regard to the duties prescribed for the slaves, this change in the law of salavery does not matter at all. It still means that a Brahmin if he was a slave, a Kshatriya if he was a slave, a Vaishya if he was a slave, did the work of a scavenger. Only a Brahmin would not do scavenging in the house of a Kshatriya, Vaishya or a Shudra. But he would do scavenging in the house of a Brahmin. Similarly, a Kshatriya would do scavening in the house of a Brahmin and the Kshatriya. Only he would not do in the house of a Vaishya or Shudra and a Vaishya would do scavenging in the house of a Brahmin, Kshatriya and Vaishya. Only he would not do it in the house of a Shudra. It is, therefore, obvious that the Brahmins, Kshatriyas and Vaishyas who are admittedly the Aryans did the work of scavengers which is the filthiest of filthy occupations. If scavenging was not loathsome to an

Aryan how can it be said that engaging in filthy occupations was the cause of Untouchability. The theory of filthy occupation as an exaplanation of Untouchability is, therefore, not tenable.

PART IV

New Theories of the Origin of Untouchability

CHAPTER IX

Contempt for Buddhists as the Root of Untouchability

I

The Census Reports for India published by the Census Commissioner at the interval of every ten years from 1870 onwards contain a wealth of information nowhere else to be found regarding the Social and religious life of the people of India. Before the Census of 1910 the Census Commissioner had a column called "Population by Religion". Under this heading the population was shown (1) Muslims, (2) Hindus, (3) Christains, etc. The Census Report for the year 1910 marked a new departure from the prevailing practice. For the first time it divided the Hindus under three separate categories, (i) Hindus, (ii) Annimists and Tribal, and (iii) the Depressed Classes or Untouchables. This new classification has been continued ever since.

II

This departure from the practice of the previous Census Commissioners raises three questions. First is what led the Commissioner for the Census of 1910 to introduce this new classification. The second is what was the criteria adopted as a basis for this classification. The third is what are the reasons for the growth of certain practices which justify the division of Hindus into three separate categories mentioned above.

The answer to the first question will be found in the address presented in 1909 by the Muslim Community under leadership of H.H. The Aga Khan to the then Viceroy, Lord Minto, in which they asked for a separate and adequate representation for the Muslim community in the legislature, executive and the public services. In the address[1]

[1] For the text of the address see my Pakistan p. 431.

there occurs the following passage :—

> "The Mohamedans of India number, according to the census taken in the year 1901 over sixty-two millions or between one-fifth and one-fourth of the total population of His Majesty's Indian dominions, *and if a reduction be made for the uncivilised portions of the community enumerated under the heads of animist and other minor religions, as well as for those classes who are ordinarily classified as Hindus but properly speaking are not Hindus at all, the proportion of Manomedans to the Hindu Majority becomes much larger.*[1] We therefore desire to submit that under any system of representation extended or limited a community in itself more numerous than the entire population of any first class European power except Russia may justly lay claim to adequate recognition as an important factor in the State.
>
> "We ventrue, indeed, with Your Excellency's permission to go a step further, and urge that the position accorded to the Mohamedan community in any kind of representation direct or indirect, and in all other ways effecting their status and influence should be commensurate, not merely with their numercial strength but also with their political importance and the value of the contribution which they make to the defence of the empire, and we also hope that Your Excellency will in this connection be pleased to give due consideration to the position which they occupied in India a little more than hundred years ago and of which the traditions have naturally not faded from their minds.

The portion in italics has a special significance. It was introduced in the address to suggest that in comprising the numerical strength of the Muslims with that of the Hindus the population of the animists, tribal and the Untouchables should be excluded. The reason for this new classification of 'Hindus' adopted by the Census Commissioner in 1910 lies in this demand of the Muslim community for separate representation on augmented scale. At any rate this is how

1. Italics not in the original.

the Hindus understood this demand.[1]

Interesting as it is the first question as to why the Census Commissioner made this departure in the system of classification is of less importance than the second question. What is important is to know the basis adopted by the Census Commissioner for separating the different classes of Hindus into (1) Those who were hundred per cent Hindus and (2) those who were not.

The basis adopted by the Census Commissioner for separation is to be found in the circular issued by the Census in which he laid down certain tests for the purpose[2] of distinguishing these two classes. Among those who were not hundred per cent Hindus were included castes and tribes which:—

(1) Deny the supremacy of the Brahmins.

(2) Do not receive the Mantra from a Brahmin or other recognized Hindu Guru.

(3) Deny the authority of the Vedas.

(4) Do not worship the Hindu gods.

(5) Are not served by good Brahmins as family priests.

(6) Have no Brahmin priests at all.

(7) Are denied access to the interior of the Hindu temples.

(8) Cause pollution (a) by touch, or (b) withen a certain distance.

(9) Bury their dead.

(10) Eat beef and do no reverence to the cow.

1. This operation came soon after the address given by Muslim community to Lord Minto in 1909 in which they asked for a separate and adequate representation for the Muslim community. The Hindu smelt a rat in it. As the Census Commissioner observed:—

"Incidentally, the enquiry generated a certain amount of heat, because unfortunately it happened to be made at a time when the rival claims of Hindus and Mohammedans to representation on the Lagislative Councils were being debated and some of the former feared that it would lead to the exclusion of certain classes from the category of Hindus and would thus react unfavourably on their political importance". Part I. p. 116.

2. See Census of India (1911). Part I. p. 117.

Out of these ten tests some divide the Hindus from the Animists and the Tribal. The rest divide the Hindus from the Untouchables. Those that divide the Untouchbles from the Hindus are (2), (5), (6), (7), and (10). It is with them that we are chiefly concerned.

For the sake of clarity it is better to divide these tests into parts and consider them separately. This Chapter will be devoted only to the consideration of (2), (5), and (6).

The replies received by the Census Commissioner to questions embodied in tests (2), (5) and (6) reveal (1) that the Untouchables do not receive the Mantra from a Brahmin; (2) that the Untouchables are not served by good Brahmin priests at all; and (3) that Untouchables have their own priests reared from themselves. On these facts the Census Commissioners of all Provinces are unanimous.[1]

Of the three questions the third is the most important. Unfortunately the Census Commissioner did not realize this. For in making his inquiries he failed to go to the root of the matter to find out: Why were the Untouchables not receiving the Mantra from the Brahmin? Why Brahmins did not serve the Untouchables as their family priests? Why do the Untouchables prefer to have their own priests? It is the 'why' of these facts which is more important than the existence of these facts. It is the 'why' of these facts which must be investigated. For the clue to the origin of Untouchability lies hidden behind it.

Before entering upon this investigation, it must be pointed out that the inquiries by the Census Commissioner were in a sense one-sided. They showed that the Brahmins shunned the Untouchables. They did not bring to light the fact that the Untouchables also shunned the Brahmins. Nonetheless, it is a fact. People are so much accustomed to thinking that the Brahmin is the superior of the Untouchables and the Untouchable accepts himself as his inferior; that this statement that the Untouchables look upon the Beahmin as an impure person is sure to come to them as a matter of

1. See Census of 1911 for Assam p.40; for Bengal, Bihar & Orisa p. 282; for C.P.p.73; for Madras p.51; for Punjab p.109; for U.P.p.121; for Baroda p.55; for Mysore p.53; for Rajputana pp.94—105; for Travancore p.198.

great surprise. The fact has however been noted by many writers who have observed and examined the social customs of the Untouchables. To remove any doubt on the point, attention is drawn to the following extracts from their writings:—

The fact was noticed by Abbe Dubois who says:-

> "Even to this day a Pariah is not allowed to pass a Brahmin Street in a village, though nobody can prevent, or prevents, his approaching or passing by a Brahmin's house in towns. The Pariahs, on their part will under no circumstances, allow a Brahmin to pass through their *paracherries* (collection of Pariah huts) as they firmly believe it will lead to their ruin".

Mr. Hemingsway, the Editor of the Gazetteer of the Tanjore District says:-[1]

> "These casts (Parayan and Pallan or Chakkiliyan castes of Tanjore District) strongly object to the entrance of a Brahmin into their quarters believing that harm will result to them therefrom".[2]

Speaking of the Holeyas of the Hasan District of Mysore, Captain J.S.F. Mackenzie says:-

> "Every village has its Holigiri ? as the quarters inhabited by the Holiars, formerly agrestic serfs, is called outside the village boundary hedge. This, I thought was because they were considered as impure race, whose touch carries defilement with it."[3]

Such is the reason generally given by the Brahmins who refuse to receive anything directly from the hands of a Holiar, and yet the Brahmins consider great luck will wait upon them if they can manage to pass through the Holigiri without being molested. To this Holiars have a strong objection, and, should a Brahmin attempt to enter their quarters, they turn out in a body and slipper him, in former times, it is said, to death. Members of the other castes may come as far as the door, but they must not enter the house, for that would bring the Holiar bad luck. If, by chance, a

1. Hindu Manners and Customs (3rd Edition) p. 61 f.n.
2. Gazetteer of Tanjore District (1906) p. 80.
3. Indian Antiquary 1073 II. 65.

person happens to get in, the owner takes care to tear the intruder's cloth, tie up some salt in one corner of it, and turn him out. This is supposed to neutralise all the good luck which might have accrued to the tresspasser, and avert any evil which ought to have befallen the owner of the house.

What is the explanation of this strange phenomenon? The explanation must of course fit in with the situation as it stood at the start, *i. e.* when the Untouchables were not Untouchables but were only Broken Men. We must ask why the Brahmins refused to officiate at the religious ceremnies of the Broken Men? Is it the case that the Brahmins refused to officiate? Or is it that the Broken Men refused to invite them? Why did the Brahmin regard Broken Men as impure? Why did the Broken Men regard the Brahmins as impure? What is the basis of this antipathy?

This antipathy can be explained on one hypothesis. It is that the Broken Men were Buddhists. As such they did not revere the Brahmins, did not employ them as their priests and regarded them as impure. The Brahmin on the other hand disliked the Broken Men because they were Buddhists and preached against them contempt and hatred with the result that the Broken Men come to be regarded as Untouchables.

We have no direct evidence that the Broken Men were Buddhists. No evidence is as a matter of fact necessary when the majority of Hindus were Buddhists. We may take it that they were.

That there existed hatred and abhorrence against the Buddhists in the mind of the Hindus and that this feeling was created by the Brahamins is not without support.

Nilkant in his *Prayaschit Mayukha*[1] quotes a verse from Manu which says:-

> "If a person touches a Buddhist or a flower of Pachupat, Lokayataka, Nastika and Mahapataki he shall purify himself by a bath."

1. Edited by Gharpure, p. 95.

The same doctrine is preached by Apararka in his Smriti.[1] Vradha Harit goes further and declares entry into the Buddhist Temple as sin requiring a purifactory bath for removing the impurity.

How widespread had become this spirit of hatred and contempt against the followers of Buddha can be observed from the science depicted in Sanskrit dramas. The most striking illustration of this attitude towards the Buddhists is to be found in the Mricchakatika. In Act VII of that Drama the hero Charudatta and his friend Maitriya are shown waiting for Vasantasena in the park outside the city. She fails to turn up and Charudatta decides to leave the park. As they are leaving, they see the Buddhist monk by name Samvahaka. On seeing him, Charudatta says :—

> "Friend Maitrya. I am anxious to meet Vasantsena... Come, let us go. (After walking a little) Ah ! here's an *inauspicious sight, a Buddhist monk* coming towards us. (After a little reflection) *well, let him come this way, we shall follow this other path.* (Exit.)

In Act VIII, the monk is in the Park of Sakara, the King's brother-in-law, washing his clothes in a pool. Sakara accompanied by Vita, turns up and threatens to kill the monk. The following conversation between them is revealing :

"Sak— Stay, you wicked monk.

Monk—Ah ! Here's the king's brother-in-law ! Because some monk has offended him, he now beats up any monk he happens to meet.

Sak— Stay, I will now break your head as one breaks a radish in a tavern. (*Beats him*).

Vita— Friend, it is not proper to beat a monk who has put on the saffron-robes, being disgusted with the world.

Monk—(*Welcomes*) Be pleased, lay brother.

Sak— Friend, see. He is abusing me.

Vita— What does he say ?

1. Smriti Sammuchaya I. p. 118.

Sak— He calls me lay brother (*upasaka*). Am I a barber ?

Vita— Oh ! He is really praising you as a devotee of the Buddha.

Sak— Why has he come here ?

Monk—To wash these clothes.

Sak— Ah ! you wicked monk. Even I myself do not bathe in this pool; I shall kill you with one stroke."

After a lot of beating, the monk is allowed to go. Here is a Buddhist Monk in the midst of the Hindu crowd. He is shunned and avoided. The feeling of disgust against him is so great that the people even shun the road the monk is travelling. The feeling of repulsion is so intense that the entry of the Buddhist was enough to cause the exit of the Hindus. The Buddhist monk is on a par with the Brahmin. A Brahmin is immune from death-penalty. He is even free from corporal punishment. But the Buddhist monk is beaten and assaulted without remorse, without compunction as though there was nothing wrong in it.

If we accept that the Broken Men were the followers of Buddhism and did not care to return to Brahmanism when it became triumphant over Buddhism as easily as other did, we have an explanation for both the questions. It explains why the Untouchables regard the Brahmins as inauspicious, do not employ them as their priest and do not even allow them to enter into their quarters. It also explains why the Broken Men came to be regarded as Untouchables. The Broken Men hated the Brahmins because the Brahmins were the enemies of Buddhism and the Brahmin imposed untouchability upon the Broken Man because they would not leave Buddhism. On this reasoning it is possible to conclude that one of the roots of untouchability lies in the hatred and contempt which the Brahmins created against those who were Buddhist.

Can the hatred between Buddhism and Brahmanism be taken to be the sole cause why Broken Men became Untouchables? Obviously, it cannot be. The hatred and contempt preached by the Brahmins was directed against

Buddhists in general and not against the Broken Men in particular. Since untouchability stuck to Broken Men only, it is obvious that there was some additional circumstance which has played its part in fastening untouchability upon the Broken Men. What that circumstance could have been ? We must next direct our effort in the direction of ascertaining it.

CHAPTER X

Beef eating as the Root of Untouchability

We now take up test No. 10 referred to in the circular issued by the Census Commissioner and to which reference has already been made in the previous chapter. The test refers to beef-eating.

The Census Returns show that the meat of the dead cow forms the Chief item of food consumed by communities which are generally classified as untouchable communities. No Hindu community, however low, will touch cow's flesh. On the other hand, there is no community which is really an Untouchable community which has not something to do with the dead cow. Some eat her flesh, some remove the skin, some manufacture articles out of her skin and bones.

From the survey of the Census Commissioner, it is well established that Untouchables eat beaf. The question however is : Has beaf-eating any relation to the origin of Untouchability ? Or is it merely an incident in the economic life of the Untouchables. Can we say that the Broken Men came to be treated as Untouchables because they ate beef ? There need be no hesitation in returning an affirmative answer to this question. No other answer is consistent with facts as we know them.

In the first place, we have the fact that the Untouchables or the main communities which compose them eat the dead cow and those who eat the dead cow are tainted with untouchability and *no others*. The co-relation between untouchability and the use of the dead cow is so great and so close that the thesis that it is the root of untouchability seems to be incontrovertible. In the second place if there is anything that separates the Untouchables from the Hindus it is beef-eating. Even a superficial view of the food taboos of the Hindus will show that there are two taboos regarding food which serve as dividing lines. There is one taboo against meat-eating. It divides Hindus into vegetarians and flesh-eaters. There is another taboo which is against beef-eating. It divides Hindus into those who eat cow's flesh and those who do not. From the point of view of untouchability the first dividing line is of no importance. But the second is. For it completely marks off the Touchables from the Untouchables. The Touchables whether they are vegetarians or flesh-eaters are united in their objection to eat cow's flesh. As against them stand the Untouchables who eat cow's flesh without compunction and as a matter of course and habit.[1]

In this context it is not far-fetched to suggest that those who have a nausea against beef-eating should treat those who eat beef as Untouchables.

There is really no necessity to enter upon any speculation as to whether beef-eating was or was not the principal reason for the rise of Untouchability. This new theory receives support from the Hindu Shastras. The Veda Vyas Smriti contains the following verse which specifies the communities which are included in the category of Antyajas and the reasons why there were so included.[2]

L. 12-13 "The *Charmakars* (Cobbler) the *Bhatta* (Soldier) the *Bhilla*, the *Rajaka* (washerman), the *Puskara*, the *Nata* (actor) the *Vrata*, the *Meda*, the *Chandala*, the *Dasa*, the *Sovapaka*, and the *Kolika*—these 'are known as Antyajas *as well as others who eat cow's flesh*."

Generally speaking the Smritikars never care to explain the why and the how of their dogmas. But this case is exception. For in this case, Veda Vyas does explain the cause of untouchability. The clause "as well as others who eat cow's flesh" is very important. It shows that the Smritikars knew that the origin of untouchablity is to be found in the eating of beef. The dictum of Veda Vyas must

1. The Untouchables have felt the force of the accusation levelled against them by the Hindus for eating beef. Instead of giving up the habit the Untouchables have invented a philosophy which justifies eating the beef of the dead cow. The gist of the philosophy is that eating the flesh of the dead cow is a better way of showing respect to the cow than throwing her carcass to the wind.

2. Quoted in Kan's History of Dharma Shastra—Vol. 11, Part 1 p. 71

close the arguement. It comes, so to say, straight from the horse's mouth and what is important is that it is also rational for it accords with facts as we know them.

The new approach in the search for the origin of Untouchability has brought to the surface two sources of the origin of Untouchability. One is the general atmosphere of scorn and contempt spread by the Brahamins against those who were Buddhists and the second is the habit of beef-eating kept on by the Broken Men. As has been said the first circumstance could not be sufficient to account for stigma of Untouchability attaching itself to the Broken Men. For the scorn and contempt for Buddhist spread by the Brahmins was too general and affected all Buddhists and not merely the Broken Men. The reason why Broken Men only became Untouchables was because in addition to being Buddhists they retained their habit of beef-eating which gave additional ground for offence to the Brahmins to carry their new-found love and reverence to the cow to its logical conclusion. We may therefore conclude that the Broken Men were exposed to scorn and contempt on the ground that they were Buddhist the main cause of their Untouchability was beef-eating.

The theory of beef-eating as the cause of untouchability also gives rise to many questions. Critics are sure to ask: What is the cause of the nausea which the Hindus have against beef-eating? Were the Hindus always opposed to beef-eating? If not, why did they develop such a nausea against it? Were the Untouchables given to beef-eating from the very start? Why did they not give up beef-eating when it was abandoned by the Hindus? Were the Untouchables always Untouchables? If there was a time when the Untouchables were not Untouchables even though they ate beef why should beef-eating give rise to Untouchability at a later-stage? If the Hindus were eating beef, when did they give it up? If Untouchability is a reflex of the nausea of the Hindus against beef-eating, how long after the Hindus had given up beef-eating did Untouchability come in to being? These questions must be answered. Without an answer to these questions, the theory will remain under cloud. It will be regarded as plausible but may not be accepted as conclusive.

Having put forth the theory, I am bound to answer these questions. I propose to take up the following heads :—

(1) Did the Hindus never eat beef ?

(2) What led the Hindus to give up beef-eating ?

(3) What led the Brahmins to become vegetarians ?

(4) Why did beef-eating give rise to Untouchability ? and

(5) When was Untouchability born ?

PART V

The New Theories and Some Questions.

CHAPTER XI

Did the Hindus Never Eat Beef ?

To the question whether the Hindus ever ate beef, every Touchable Hindu, whether he is a Brahmin or a non-Brahmin, will say 'no, never.' In a certain sense, he is right. From times no Hindu has eaten beef. If this is all that the Touchable Hindu wants to convey by his answer there need be no quarrel over it. But when the learned Brahmins argue that the Hindus not only never ate beef but that they always held the cow to be sacred and were always opposed to the killing of the cow, it is impossible to accept their view.

What is the evidence in support of the construction that the Hindus never ate beef and were opposed to the killing of the cow ?

There are two series of references in the Rig Veda on which reliance is placed. In one of these, the cow is spoken of as *Aghnya.* They are Rig Veda 1. 164,27; IV. 1.6 ; V.82-8 ; VII. 69 71 ; X.87. *Aghnya* means 'one who does not deserve to be killed.' From this, it is argued that this was a prohibition against the killing of the cow and that since the Vedas are the final authority in the matter of religion, it is concluded that the Aryans could not have killed the cows, much less could they have eaten beef. In another series of references the cow is spoken of as sacred. They are Rig Veda VI.28.1.8. and VIII.10115. In these verses the cow is addressed as Mother of Rudras, the Daughter of Vasus, the Sister of the Adityas and the Centre of Nectar. Another reference on the subject is in Rig Veda VIII.101.16 where the cow is called Devi (Goddess).

Raliance is also placed on certain passages in the Brahmanas and Sutras.

There are two passages in the Satapatha Brahmana which relate to animal sacrifice and beef-eating. One is at III. 1.2.21 and reads as follows :—

> " He (the Adhvaryu) then makes him enter the hall. Let him not eat (the flesh) of either the

cow or the ox, for the cow and the ox doubtless support everything here on earth. The goods spake, 'verily, the cow and the ox support everything here; come, let us bestow on the cow and the ox whatever vigour belonged to other species (of animals); and therefore the cow and the ox eat most. Hence were one to eat (the flesh) of an ox or a cow, there would be, as it were, an eating of everything, or, as it were, a going to the end (or, to destruction)... Let him therefore not eat (the flesh) of the cow and the ox."

The other passage is at 1, 2, 3, 6. It speaks against animal sacrifice and on ethical grounds.

A similar statement is contained in the Apastambha Dharma Sutra at 1. 5. 17, 29. Apastambha lays a general embargo on the eating or cow's flesh.

Such is vidence in support of the contention that the Hindus never ate beef. What conclusion can be drawn from this evidence ?

So far as the evidence from the Rig Veda is concerned the conclusion is based on a misreading and misunderstanding of the texts. The adjective Aghnya applied to the cow in the Rig Veda means a cow that was yielding milk and therefore not fit for being killed. That the cow is venerated in the Rig Veda is of course true. But this regard and venerations of the cow are only to be expected from an agricultural community like the Indo-Aryans. This application of the utility of the cow did not prevent the Aryan from killing the cow for purposes of food. Indeed the cow was killed because the cow was regarded as sacred. As observed by Mr. Kane:

> "It was not that the cow was not sacred in Vedic times, it was because of her sacredness that it is ordained in the Vajnasaneyi Samhita that beef should be eaten."[1]

That the Aryans of the Rig Veda did kill cows for purposes of food and ate beef is abundantly clear from the Rig Veda itself. In Rig Veda (X. 86. 14) Indra says:—"They

1. Dharma Shastra Vichar (Marathi) p. 180.

cook for one 15 plus twenty oxen. The Rig Veda (X. 91. 14) says that for Agni were sacrificed horses, bulls, oxen, barren cows and rams. From the Rig Veda (X. 72. 6) it appears that the cow was killed with a sword or axe.

As to the testimony of the Satapatha Bramhana, can it be said to be conclusive? Obviously, it cannot be. For there are passages in the other Bramhanas which give a different opinion.

To give only one instance. Among the Kamyashtis set forth in the Taittiriya Bramhana, not only the sacrifice of oxen and cows are laid down, but we are even told what kind and description of oxen and cow are to be offered to what dieties. Thus, a dwarf ox is to be chosen for sacrifice to Vishnu; a drooping horned bull with a blaze on the forehead to Indra as the destroyer of Vrita; a black cow to Pushan; a red cow to Rudra; and so on. The Taithiriya Bramhana notes another sacrifice called *Panchasaradiya-seva*, the most important element of which was the immolation of seventeen five-year old humpless, dwraf-bulls, and as many dwarf heifers under three year-old.

As against the statement of the Apasthamba Dharma Sutra, the following points may be noted.

First is the contrary statement contained in that Very Sutra, At I.5,14,29, the Sutra says:-

> "The cow and the bull are sacred and therefore should be eaten".

The second is the prescription of Madhuparka contained in the Grahya Sutras. Among the Aryans the etipuette for receiving important guests had become settled in to custom and had become a ceremony. The most important offering was Madhupark. A Detailed descriptions regarding Madhuparka are to be found in the various Grahya Sutras. According to most of the Grahya Sutras there are six persons who have a right to be served with Madhuparka namely, (1) Ritwija or the Brahmin called to perform a a sacrifice, (2) Acharya the teacher, (3) The bridegroom (4) The King (5) The Snatak, the student who has just finished his studies at the Gurukul and (6) Any person who is dear to the host. Some add Atithi to this list. Except in the case of Ritvija, King and Acharya Madhuparka is to be offered to the rest once in a year. To the Ritvija, King and Acharya it is to be offered each time they come.

What was this Madhuparka made of ? There is divergence about the substances mixed in offering Madhuparka. Asv.gr and Ap.gr. (13. 10) prescribe a mixture of honey and curds or clarified butter and curds. Others like Par.gr.13 prescribe a mixture of three (curds, honey and butter). Ap. gr. (13.11-12) states the view of some that those three may be mixed or five (those three with fried yava grain and barley). Hir.gr.I.,1210-12 give the option of mixing three of five (curds, honey, ghee, water and ground grain). The Kausika Sûtra (92) speaks of nine kinds of mixtures, *viz.*, Brahma (honey and curds). Aindra (of payasa), Saumya (curds and ghee), Pausna (ghee and mantha), Sarasvata (milk and ghee), Mausala (wine and ghee, this being used only in Sautramanai and Rajasuya sacrifices), Parivrajaka (sesame oil and oil cake). The Madava gr.I.9.22 says that the veda declares that the Madhuparka must not be without flesh and so it recommends that if the cow is let loose, goat's meat or payase (rice cookad in milk) may be offered; the Hir.gr. 1.13. 14 says that other meat should be offered; Baud.gr. (1.2,51-54) says that when the cow is let off the flesh of a goat or ram may be offered or some forest flesh (of a deer, etc.) may be offered, as there can be no Madhuparka without flesh or if one is unable to offer flesh one may cook ground grains.

Thus the essential element in Madhuparka is flesh and particularly cow's flesh.

The killing of cow for the guest had grown to such an extent that the guest came to be called 'Go-gnha' which means the killer of the cow. To avoid this slaughter of the cows the Ashvalayana Grahya Sutra (1.24.25) suggests that the cow should be let loose when the guest comes so as to escape the rule of etiquette.

Thirdly, reference may be to the ritual relating to disposal of the dead to counter the testimony of the Apastambha Dharma Sutra. The Sutra says:-

1. Kane's vol. II. Part I p.545

"1. He should then put the following (sacrificial) implements (on the deadbody).

2. Into the right hand the (spoon called) Guhu.

3. Into the left the (other spoon called) Upabhrit.

4. On his right side the wooden sacrificial sword called Sphya, on his left side the Agnihotrahavani (*i.e.*, the laddle with which the Agnihotra oblations are sacrificed).

5. On his chest the (big sacificial laddle called) Dhruva. On his head the dishes. On his teeth the pressing stones

6. On the two sides of his nose the two smaller sacrificial laddles called Sruvas.

7. Or, if there is only one (Sruva), breaking it (in two pieces).

8. On his two ears the two Prasitraharanas (*i.e*, the vessels into which the portion of the sacrificial food belonging to the Brahmin) is put

9. Or, if there is only one (Prasitraharana), breaking it (in two pieces).

10 On his belly the (vessel called) Patri.

11 And the cup into which the cut-off portion (of the sacrificial food) are put.

12. On his secret parts the (staff called) Samya.

'13. On his thighs two kindling woods.

'14. On his legs the mortar and the pestle.

15. On his feet the two baskets.

16. Or, if there is only one(basket), bearing it in two pieces.

17. Those of the implements which have a hollow (into which liquids can be poured) are filled with sprinkled butter.

18. The son (of the deceased person) should take the under and the upper mill-stone for himself.

19. And the implements made of copper, iron and earthenware.

20. Taking out the omentum of the she-animal he should cover therewith the head and the mouth (of the dead person) with the verse, 'But on the armour (which will protect thee) against Agni, by that which comes from the cows.' (Rig Ved.X.16.7.

21. Taking out the kidneys of the animal he should lay them into the hands (of the dead body) with the verse escape the two hounds, the sons of Sarma (Rig Veda X 1410) the right kidney into the right hand and the left into the left hand.

22. The heart of the animals he puts on the heart of the deceased.

23. And two lumps of flour or rice according to some teachers.

24. Only if there are no kidneys according to some teachers.

25. Having distributed the whole (animal), limb by limb (placing its different limbs on the corresponding limbs of the deceased) and having covered it with its hide, he recites when the Pranita water is carried forward (the verse), 'Agni' do not overturn this cup. (Rig Veda, X.16.8).

26. Bending his left knee he should sacrifice Yugya oblation into the Dakshina fire with the formulas 'To Agni Svahai; to Kama Svaha To the world Svaha to Anumati Svaha'.

27. A fifth (oblation) on the chest of the deceased with the formula 'from this one verily thouhast been born. May he now be born out of thee. To the heaven worlds avaha,."

From the above passage quoted from the Ashvalayan Grahya Sutra it is clear that among the ancient Indo-Aryans when a person died an animal had to be killed and the parts of the animal were placed on the appropriate parts of the deadbody before the deadbody was burned.

Such is the state of the evidence on the subject of cow-killing and beef-eating. Which part of it is to be accepted as true? The correct view is that the testimony of the Satapatha Brahmana and the Apastambha Dharma Sutra in so far as it supports the view that Hindus were against cow-killing and beef-eating, are merely exhortation against the excesses of cow-killing and not prohibitions against cow-killing. Indeed the exhortations prove that cow-killing and eating of beef had become a common practice. That notwithstanding these exhortations cow-killing and beef-eating continued. That most often they fell on deaf ears is proved by the conduct of Yajnavalkya, the great Rishi of the Aryans. The first passage quoted above from the Satapatha Brahmana was really addressed to Yajnavalkya as an exhortation. How did Yajnavalkya respond? After listening to the exhotation this is what Yajnavalkya said:-

"I, for one, eat it, provided that it is tender"

That the Hindus at one time did kill cows and did eat beef is proved abundantly by the description of the Yajnas given in the Buddhist Sutras which relate to periods much later than the Vedas and the Brahmanas. The scale on which the slaughter of cows and animals took place was collosal. It is not possible to give a total of such slaughter on all accounts committed by the Brahmins in the name of religion. Some idea of the extent of this slaughter can however be had from references to it in the Buddhist literature. As an illustration refernce may be made to the Kutadanta Sutta in which Buddha preached against the performance of animal sacrifices to Brahmin Kutadanta. Buddha though speaking in a tone of sarcastic travesty gives a good idea of the practices and rituals of the Vedic sacrifices when he said:

> " And further, O Brahmin, at that sacrifice neither were any oxen slain, neither goats, nor fowls, nor fatted pigs, nor were any kind of living creatures put to death. No trees were cut down to be used as posts, no Darbha grasses mowen to stress round the sacrificial spot. And the slaves and messengers and workmen there employed were driven neither by rods nor

> fear, nor carried on their work weeping with tears upon their faces."

Kutadanta on the other hand in thanking Buddha for his conversion gives an idea of the magnitude of the slaughter of animals which took place at such sacrifices when he says:-

> "I, even I, betake myself to the venerable Gotama as my guide, to the Doctrine and the Order, May the venerable One accept me as a disciple, as one who, from this day forth, as long as life endures, has taken him as his guide, and I myself, O, Gotama, will have the seven hundred bulls, and the seven hundred steers, and the seven hundred heifers, and the seven hundred goats, and the seven hundred rams set free. To thee I grant their life. Let them eat grass and drink fresh water and may cool breezes waft round them."

In the Samyuta Nikaya (III,1-9) we have another description of a Yajna performed by Pasenadi, king of Kosala. It is said that five hundred bulls, five hundred calves and many heifers, goats and rams were led to the pillar to be sacrificed.

With this evidence no one can doubt that there was a time when Hindus-both Brahmins and non--Brahmins ate not only flesh but also beef.

CHAPTER XII

Why Did Non-Brahmins give up Beef-eating ?

The food habits of the different classes of Hindus heve been as fixed and stratified as their cults. Just as Hindus can be classified on their basis of their cults so also they can be classified on the basis of their habits of food. On the basis of their cults, Hindus are either *Saivites* (followers of Siva) or *Vaishnavites* (followers of Vishnu). Similarly, Hindus are either Mansahari (those who eat flesh) or Shakahari (those who are vegitarians).

For ordinary purposes the division of Hindus into two classes *Mansahari* and *Shakahari* may be enough. But it must be admitted that it is not exhaustive and does not take account of all the classes which exist in Hindu society. For an exhaustive classification, the class of Hindus called *Manssahari* shall have to be further divided into two sub-clas es (i) Those who eat flesh but do not eat cow's flesh; and (ii) Those who eat flesh including caw's flesh. In other words, on the basis of food taboos, Hindu society follows into three classes: (i) Those who are vegetarians; (ii) Those who eat flesh but do not eat cow's flesh; and (iii) Those who eat flesh including cow's flesh. Corresponding to this classification, we have in Hindu society three classes: (1) Brahmins; (2) Non-Brahmins; and (3) The Untouchables. This division though not in accord with the fourfold division of society called Chaturvarnya, yet it is in accord with facts as they exist. For, in the Brahmins[1] we have a class which is vegetarian, in the non-Brahmins the class which eats flesh but does not eat cow's flesh and in the Untouchables a class which eats flesh including cow's flesh.

This threefold division is therefore substantial and is in accord with facts. Anyone who spots to turn over this classification in his mind is bound to be struck by the position of

1. The Brahmins of India fall into two divisions (1) Pancha Dravid and (2) Panch Ganda The former are vegetarians, the later are not.

the Non-Brahmins. One can quite understand vegetarianism. One can quite understand meat-eating. But it is difficult to understand why a person who is a flesh-eater should object to one kind of flesh namely cow's flesh. This is an anamoly which call for explanation. Why did the Non-Brahmin give up beef-eating? For this purpose it is necessary to examine laws on the subject. The relevant legislation must be found either in the Law of Asoka or the Law of Manu.

II

To begin with Asoka. The edicts of Asoka which have reference to this matter are Rock Edict No. I and Pillar Edicts Nos.II and V. Rock Edict No.I read as follows:-

> "This pious Edict has been written by command of His Sacred and Gracious Majesty the King. Here (in the capital) no animal may be slaughtered for sacrifice, nor may the holiday feast be held, because His Sacred and Gracious Majesty the king sees much offence in the holiday feasts, although in certain places holiday feasts are excellent in the sight of His Sacred and Gracious Majesty the king.
>
> "Formerly, in the kitchen of His Sacred and Gracious Majesty the King each day many hundred thousands of living creatures were slaughtered to make curries, But now, when this pious edict is being written, only three living creatures are slaughtered (daily) for curry, to wit, two peacocks and one antelope: the antelope, however, not invariably. Even those three living creatures henceforth shall not be slaughtered."

Pillar Edict No.II was in the following terms:-

"Thus saith His Sacred and Gracious Majesty the King:-

"The Law of piety is excellent. But wherein consists the Law of Piety? In these things, to wit, little impiety, many good deeds, compassion, liberality, truthfulness and purity.

The gift of spiritual insight I have given in manifold ways: whilst on two-footed and four-footed beings, on birds and the denizens of the waters. I have conferred various favours-even unto the boon of life; and many other good deed have I done.

For this my purpose, have I caused this pious edict to be written, that men may walk after its teaching, and that it may long endure; and he who will follow its teaching will do well."

Pillar Edict V says :-

"Thus said His Sacred and Gracious Majesty, the king:

When I had been consecrated twentv-six years the following species were declared *exempt from slaughter*, namely:-

Parrots, starkings(?) adjutants, Brahmany ducks, geese *pandimukhas, gelatas*, bats, queen-ants, female tortosises, boneless fish, *vedaveyakas, gangapuputakas*, skate, (river) tortoise, porcupines tree-squirrels, barasingha stage, Brahmany bulls monkeys, rhinocerous, grey doves village piegeons, and *all four-footed animals which are not utillised or eaten.*

She-goats, ewes, sows, that is to say, those either with young or in milk, are exempt from slaughter as well as their off-spring up to six months of age.

The caponing of cocks must not be done.

Chaff must not be burned along with the living things in it.

Forests must not be burned either for mischief or so as to destroy living creatures.

The living must not be fed with the living. At each of the three seasonal full moons, and at the full moon of the month Tishya (December-January) for three days in each case, namely, the fourteenth and fifteenth days of the first fortnight, and the first day of the second fortnight, as well as on the first days throughout, the year, fish is exempt from killing and may not be sold.

"On the same days, in elephant-preserves or fish-ponds no other classes of animals may be destroyed.

On the eighth, fourteenth and fifteenth days of each fortnight, as well as on the Tishya and Punarvasa days and festival days, the castration of bulls must not be performed, nor may he-goats, rams, boars and other animals liable to castration be castrated.

On the Tishya and Punarvasa days, on the seasonal full-moon days, and during the fortnights of the seasonal full moons the branding of horses and oxen must not be done.

During the time up to the twenty-sixth anniversary of my consecration twenty-five jail deliveries have been effected." So much for the legislation of Asoka."

III

Let us turn to Manu. His Laws contain the following provisions regarding meat-eating:-

"V.11. Let him avoid all carnivorous birds and those living in villages, and one-hoofed animals which are not specially permitted (to be eaten). and the Tithbha (Parra) Jacana.

V.12. The sparrow, the Plava, the Hamsa, the Brahmani duck the village-cock, the Sarasa crane, the Reggudala, the wood-pecker, the parrot, and the starling.

V.13. Those which feed striking with their beaks, web-footed birds, the Koyashti, those which scratch with their toes, those which dive and live on fish, meat from a slaughter-house and dried meat.

V.14. The Baka and the Balaka crane, the raven, the Khangartaka(animals) that eat fish, village-pigs, and all kind of fishes.

V.15. He who eats the flesh of any (animals) is called the eater of the flesh of that (particular) creature, he who eats flesh is an eater of every (kind of) flesh; let him therefore avoid fish.

V.16. (But the fish called) Pathine and (that called) Rohita may be eaten, if used for offering to the gods or to the manes (one may eat) likewise Ragivas, Simhatundas, and Sasalkas on all occasions.

V.17. Let him not eat solitary or unknown beasts and bird,s though they my fall under (the categories of) eatable creatures, not any five-footed animal.

V.18. The porcupine,the hedgehog, the iguana, the rhinoceros, the tortoise, and the hare they declare to be eatable; likewise those domestic animals that have teeth in one jaw excepting camels."

IV

Here is survey of the legislation both by Asoka and by Manu on the slaughter of animals. We are of course principally concerned with the cow. Examining the legislation of Asoka the question is: Did he prohibit the killing of the cow? On this issue there seem to be a difference of opinion. Prof. Vincent Smith is of opinion that Asoka did not prohibit the killing of the cow. Commenting on the legislation of Asoka on the subject Prof. Smith says:[1]

> "It is noteworthy that Asoka's rules do not forbid the slaughter of cow, which, apparently, continued to be lawful."

Prof. Radhakmud Mookerji joins issue with Prof. Smith and says[2] that Asoka did prohibit the slaughter of the cow. Prof Mookerji relies upon the reference in Pillar Edict V to the rule of exemption which was made applicable to all four-footed animals and argues that under this rule cow was exempced from killing. This is not a correct readring of the statement in the Edict. The Statement in the Edict is a qualified statement. It does not refer to all four-footed animals but only to four-footed animals, '*which are not utilized or eaten.*" A cow cannot be said to be a four-footed animal which was not utilized or eaten. Prof. Vincent Smith seems to be correct in saying that Asoka did not prohibit the slaughter of the cow. Prof. Mookerji tries to get out of the difficulty by saying that at the time of Asoka the cow was not eaten and therefore came within the prohibition. His statement is simply absurd for the cow was an animal which was very much eaten by all class.

It is quite unnecessary to resort as does Prof. Mookerji to a forced construction of the Edict and to make Asoka prohibit the slaughter of the cow as though it was his duty to do so. Asoka had no particular interest in the cow and owed no special duty to protect her against killing. Asoka was interested in the sanctity of all life human as well as animal. He felt his duty to prohibit the taking of life where taking of life was not necessary. That is why he prohibited slaughter of animal for sacrifice[3] which he regarded as unnecessary

1, Asoka p. 58. 2. Asoka pp. 21,181,184. 3. See Rock Edict No. 1.

and of animals which are not utilized nor eaten which again would be wanton and unnecessary. That he did not prohibit the slaughter of the cow in specie may well be taken as a fact which for having regard to the Buddhist attitude in the matter cannot be used against Asoka as a ground for casting blame.

Coming to Manu there is no doubt that he too did not prohibit the slaughter of the cow. On the other hand he made the eating of cow's flesh on certain occasions obligatory.

Why then did the non-Brahmins give up eating beef ? There appears to be no apparent reason for this departure on their part. But there must be some reason behind it. The reason I like to suggest is that it was due to their desire to imitate the Brahmins that the non-Brahmins gave up beef-eating. This may be a novel theory but it is not an impossible theory. As the French author, Gabriel Tarde has explained culture within a society spreads by imitations of the ways and manners of the superior classes by the inferior classes. This imitation is so regular in its flow that its working is as mechanical as the working of a natural law. Gabriel Tarde speaks of the laws of imitations. One of these laws is that the lower classes always imitate the higher classes. This is a matter of such common knowledge that hardly any individual can be found to question its validity.

That the spread of the cow-worship among and cessation of beaf-eating by the non-Brahmins has taken place by reason of the habit of the non-Brahmins to imitate the Brahmins who were undoubtedly their superiors is beyond dispute. Of course there was an extensive propaganda in favour of cow-worship by the Brahmins. The Gayatri Purana is a piece of this propaganda. But initially it is the result of the natural law of imitation. This, of course, raises another question: Why did the Brahmins give up beef-eating ?

CHAPTER XIII

What Made the Brahmins Become Vegetarians ?

The non-Brahmins have evidently undergone a revolution. From being beef-eaters to have become non-beef-eaters was indeed a revolution. But if the non-Brahmins underwent one revolution, the Brahmins had undergone two. They gave up beef-eating which was one revolution. To have given up meat-eating altogether and become vegetarians was another revolution.

That this was a revolution is beyond question. For as has been shown in the previous chapters there was a time when the Brahmins were the greatest beef-eaters. Although the non-Brahmins did eat beef they could not have had it every day. The cow was a costly animal and the non-Brahmins could ill afford to slaughter it just for food. He only did it on special occasion when his religious duty or personal interest to propitiate a deity compelled him to do. But the case with the Brahmin was different. He was a priest. In a period overridden by ritualism there was hardly a day on which there was no cow sacrifice to which the Brahmin was not invited by some non-Brahmin. For the Brahmin every day was a beef-steak day. The Brahmins were therefore the greatest beef-eaters. The Yajna of the Brahmins was nothing but the killing of innocent animals carried on in the name of religion with pomp and ceremony with an attempt to enshroud it in mystery with a view to conceal their appetite for beef. Some idea of this mystery pomp and ceremony can be had from the directions contained in the Atreya Brahamana touching the killing of animals in a Yajna.

The actual killing of the animal is preceded by certain Initiatory Rites accompanied by incantations too long and too many to be detailed here. It is enough to give an idea of the main features of the Sacrifice. The Sacrifice commences with the erection of the Sacrificial post called the Yupa to which the animal is tied before it is slaughtered.

After setting out why the Yupa is necessary the Atreya Brahamana proceeds to state what it stands for. It says:[1]

> "This Yupa is a weapon. Its point must have eight edges. For a weapon (or iron club) has eight edges. Whenever he strikes with it an enemy or adversary, he kills him. (This weapon serves) to put down him (every one) who is to be put down by him (the sacrificer). The Yupa is a weapon which stands erected (being ready) to slay an enemy. Thence an enemy (of the sacrificer) who might be present (at the sacrifice) comes of all ill after having seen the Yupa of such or such one."

The selection of the wood to be used for the Yupa is made to vary with the purposes which the sacrificer wishes to achieve by the sacrifice. The Atreya Brahamana says:

"He who desires heaven, ought to make his Yupa of Khadira wood. For the gods conquered the celestial world by means of a Yupa, made of Khadira wood. In the same way the sacrificer conquers the celestial world by means of a Yupa, made of Khadira wood.

"He who desires food and wishes to grow fat ought to make his Yupa of Bilva wood. For the Bilva tree bears fruits every year; it is the symbol of fertility; for it increases (every year) in size from the roots up to the branches, therefore it is a symbol of fatness. He who having such a knowledge makes his Yupa of Bilva wood, makes fat his children and cattle.

"As regards the Yupa made of Bilva wood (it is further to be remarked), that they call 'light' Bilva. He who has such a knowledge becomes a 'light' among his own people, the most distinguished among his own people.

"He who desires beauty and sacred knowledge ought to make his Yupa of Palasa wood. For the Palasa is among the trees of beauty and sacred knowledge. He who having such a knowledge makes his Yupa of Palasa wood, becomes beautiful and acquires sacred knowledge.

1. Atreya Brahamana II pp. 72-74.

"As regards the Yupa made of Palasa wood (there is further to be remarked), that the Palasa is the womb of all trees. Thence they speak on account of the palasam (foliage) of this or that tree (i.e. they call the foliage of every tree palasam). He who has such a knowledge obtains (the gratification of) any desire, he might have regarding all trees (i.e. he obtains from all trees any thing he might wish for)."

This is followed by the ceremony of anointing the sacrificial post[1].

"The Adhvaryu says (to the Hotar): "We anoint the sacrificial post (Yupa); repeat the mantrâ (required)". The Hotar then repeats the verse: "Amjanti tvam adhvare" (3,8,1), i.e. "The priests anoint thee, O tree! with celestial honey (butter); provide (us) with wealth if thou standest here erected, or it thou art lying on thy mother (earth)." The "celestial honey" is the melted butter (with which the priests anoint the Yupa). (The second half verse from) " provide us " &c. means: "thou mayest stand or lie, provide us with wealth."

"(The Hotar then repeats:) "jato jayate sudinatve" &c. (3,8,5.) i.e. "After having been born, he (the Yupa) is growing (to serve) in the prime of his life the sacrifice of mortal men. The wise are busy in decorating (him, the Yupa) with skill. He, as an eloquent messenger of the gods, lifts his voice (that it might be heard by the gods)." He (the Yupa) is called jata, i. e. born, because he is born by this (by the recital of the first quarter of this verse). (By the word) vardhamana, i.e growing, they make him (the Yupa) grow in this manner. (By the words:) punanti (i.e. to clean, decorate), they clean him in this manner. (By the words:) "he as an eloquent messenger, &c." he announces the Yupa (the fact of his existence) to the gods.

1. Atreya Brahmana (Martin Haug) II pp. 74-78

The Hotar then concludes (the ceremony of anointing the sacrificial post) with the verse "yuva suvasah parivitah" (3,8,4.), i e. "the youth decorated with ribands, has arrived; he is finer (than all trees) which ever grew; the wise priests raise him up under recital of well-framed thoughts of their mind." The youth decorated with ribands, is the vital air (the soul), which is covered by the limbs of the body. (By the words:) "he is finer," &c. he means that he (the Yupa) is becoming finer (more excellent, beautiful) by this (mantra)."

The next ceremony is the carrying of fire round the sacrificial animal. The Atreya Brahmana gives the following directions on this point. It says[1] :--

> "When the fire is carried round (the animal) the Adhvaryu says to the Hotar: repeat (thy mantras). The Hotar then repeats this triplet of verses, addressed to Agni, and composed in the Gayatri metre: *Agnir Hota no adhvare* (4.15.1-3) i.e (1) Agni, our priest, is carried round about like a horse, he who is among gods the god of sacrifices. (2) Like a charioteer Agni passes thrice by the sacrifice: to the gods he carries the offering. (3) The master of food, the seer of Agni, went round the offering; he bestows riches on the :
>
> "When the fire is carried round (the animal) then he makes him (Agni) prosper by means of his own deity and his own metre. 'As a horse he is carried' means: they carry him as if he were a horse, round about. Like a charioteer Agni passes thrice by the sacrifice means: he goes round the sacrifice like a charioteer (swiftly). He is called *vajapati* (master of food) because he is the master of (different kinds of) food.
>
> "*The Advaryu says* : give Hotar ! the additional order for despatching offerings to the gods.
>
> "*The Hotar then says* (to the slaughterers) : Ye divine slaughterers, commence (your work), as well as ye who are human ! that is to say, he orders all the slaughterers among gods as well as among men (to commence).
> Bring hither the instruments for killing, ye who are ordering the sacrifice, in behalf of the two masters of the sacrifice.

1. Atreya Brahmana (Martin Haug) II - pp. 84-86.

"The animal is the offering, the sacrificer the master of the offering. Thus he (the Hotar) makes prosper the sacrificer by means of his (the sacrificer's) own offering. Thence they truly say : for whatever deity the animal is killed, that one is the master of the offering. If the animal is to be offered to one deity only, the priest should say : Medhapataye 'to the master of the sacrifice (singular)'; if to two deities, then he should use the dual 'to both masters of the offering', and if to several deities, then he should use the plural, 'to the masters of the offering'. This is the established custom.

Bring ye for him fire! For the animal when carried (to the slaughter) saw death before it. Not wishing to go to the gods, the gods said to it : Come, we will bring thee to heaven ! The animal consented and said : One of you should walk before me. They consented. Agni then walked before it, and it followed after Agni. Thence they say, every animal belongs to Agni, for it followed after him. Thence they carry before the animal fire (Agni).

Spread the (sacred) grass! The animal lives on herbs. H (the Hotar) thus provides the animal with its entire sou (the herbs being supposed to form part of it).

After the ceremony of carrying fire round the anim comes the delivery of the animal to the priests for sacrific Who should offer the animal for sacrifice? On this point th direction of the Atreya Brahmana is[1]-

"*The mother, the father, the brother, sister, friend, and companions should give this (animal) up (for being slaughtered)* ! When these words are pronounced, they seize the animal which is (regarded as) entirely given up by its relations (parents, &c.)".

On reading this direction one wonders why almost ever body is required to join in offering the animal for sacrifi The reason is simple. There were altogether seventeen Bra min priests who were entitled to take part in performing t

1 Atreya Brahmana (Martin Haug) II p. 86.

sacrifice. Naturally enough they wanted the whole carcass to themselves.[1] Indeed they could not give enough to each of the seventeen priests unless they had the whole carcass to distribute. Legally the Brahmins could not claim the whole carcass unless everybody who could not claim any right over the animal had been divested of it. Hence the direction requiring even the companion of the sacrificer to take part in offering the animal.

Then comes the ceremony of actually killing the animal. The Atreya Brahamana gives the details of the mode and manner of killing the animal. Its directions are[2]—

> "Turn its feet northwards! Make its eye go to the sun, dismiss its breath to the wind, its life to the air, its hearing to the directions, its body to the earth. In this way he (the Hotar) places it (connects it) with these worlds.
>
> *Take off the skin entire* (*without cutting it*). *Before opening the naval, tear out omentum. Stop its breathing within* (by stopping its mouth). Thus he (the Hotar) puts its breath in the animals.
>
> *Make of its breast a piece like an eagle, of its arms* (two pieces like) *two hatchets, of its forearms* (two pieces like) *two spikes, of its shoulders* (two pieces like) *two Kashyapas, its loins should be un-broken* (entire) ; (make of) *its thighs* (two pieces like) *two shields, of the two kneepans* (two pieces like) *two oleander leaves ; take out its twentysix ribs according to their order; preserve every limb of it in its integrity*. Thus he benefits all its limbs."

There remain two ceremonies to complete the sacrificial killing of the animal. One is to absolve the Brahmin priests who played the butcher's part. Theoretically they are guilty of murder for the animal is only a substitute for the sacrificer. To absolve them from the consequences of murder, the Hotar is directed by the Atreya Brahamana to observe the following injunction[3] :

1. As a matter of fact the Brahmins took the whole carcass. Only one leg each was given to the sacrificer and his wife.
2. Atreya Brahmana (Martin Haug) II pp 86-87.
3. Ibid pp. 88-90

"*Do not cut the entrails which resemble an owl* (when taking out the omentum), *nor should among your children, O slaughterers! or among their offspring any one be found who might cut them.* By speaking these words he presents these entrails to the slaughterers among the gods as well as to those among men.

The Hotar shall then say thrice: O *Adhrigu* (and ye others), *kill* (the animal), *do it well*; kill it, O *Adhrigu.*

After the animal has been killed, (he should say thrice:) *Far may it* (the consequences of murder) be (from us). For Adhrigu among the gods is he who silences (the animal) and the *Apapa* (away, away!) is he who puts it down. By speaking those words he surrenders the animal to those who silence it (by stopping its mouth) and to those who butcher it.

The Hotar then mutters (he makes *Japa*); "O slaughterers! may all good you might do abide by us! and all mischief you might do go elsewhere!" The Hotar gives by (this) speech the order (for killing the animal), for Agni had given the order for killing (the animal) with the same words when he was the Hotar of the gods.

By those words (the *Japa* mentioned) the Hotar removes (all evil consequences) from those who suffocate the animal and those who butcher it, in all that they might transgress the rule by cutting one piece too soon, the other too late, or by cutting a too large, or a too small piece. The Hotar enjoying this happiness clears himself (from all guilt) and attains the full length of his life (and it serves the sacrificer) for obtaining his full life. He who has such a knowledge, attains the full length of his life."

The Atreya Bramhana next deals with the question of disposing of the parts of the dead animal. In this connection its direction is[1]—

1. Atreya Brahmana (Martin Haug) II p. 87

"*Dig a ditch in the earth to hide its excrements.* The excrements consist of vegetable food; for the earth is the place for the herbs. Thus the Hotar puts them (the excrements) finally in their proper places. *Present the evil spirits with the blood!* For the gods having deprived (once) the evil spirits of their share in the Haviryajnas (such as the Full and New Moon offerings) apportioned to them the husks and smallest grains, and after having them turned out of the great sacrifice (such as the *Soma* and animal sacrifices), presented to them the blood. Thence the Hotar pronounces the words: *present the evil spirits with the blood!* By giving them this share he deprives the evil spirits of any other share in the sacrifice. They say: one should not address the evil spirits in the sacrifice, and evil spirits whichever they might be (Rakshasas, Asuras etc.); for the sacrifice is to be without (the) evil spirits (not to be disturbed by them). But others say: one should address them; for (he) who deprives anyone, "entitled to a share, of this share, will be punished (by him whom he deprives); and if he himself does not suffer the penalty, then his son, and if his son be spared, then his grandson will suffer it, and thus he resents on him (the son or grandson) what he wanted to resent on you."

"However, if the Hotar addresses them, he should do so with a low voice. For both, the low voice and the evil spirits, are, as it were, hidden. If he addresses them with a loud voice, then such one speaks in the voice of the evil spirits, and is capable of producing Rakshasa sounds (a horrible, terrific voice). The voice in which the haughty man and the drunkard speak is that of the evil spirits (Rakshasas). He who has such a knowledge will neither himself become haughty nor will such a man be among his offspring."

Then follows the last and the concluding ceremony -- that of offering parts of the body of the animal to the gods.

It is called the Manota. According to the Atreya Brahamana[1]—

> "The Adhvaryu says (to the Hotar): recite the verses appropriate to the offering of the parts of the sacrificial animal which are cut off for the Manota. He then repeats the hymn : Thou, O Agni, art the first Manota[2] (6.1)"

There remains the question of sharing the flesh of the animal. On this issue the division was settled by the Atreya Brahamana in the following terms[3] :

> "Now follows the division of the different parts of the sacrificial animal (among the priests). We shall describe it. The two jawbones with the tongue are to be given to the Prastotar; the breast in the form of an eagle to the Udgatar; the throat with the palate to the Pratihartar; the lower part of the right loins to the Hotar ; the left to the Brahma ; the right thigh to the Maitravaruna ; the left to the Brahmanachhamsi ; the right side with the shoulder to the Adhvaryu ; the left side to those who accompany the chants ; the left shoulder to the Pratipashatar; the lower part of the right arm to the Neshtar; the lower part of the left arm to the Potar; the upper of of the right thigh to the Achhavaka; the left to the Agnidhara ; the upper part of the right arm to the Atreya ; the left to the Sadasya; the back bone and the urinal bladder to the Grihapati (sacrificer); the right feet to the Grihapati who gives a feasting; the left feet to the wife of that Grihapati who gives a feasting; the upper lip is common to both (the Grihapati and his wife), which is to be divided by the Grihapati. They offer the tail of the animal to wives, but they should give it to a Brahmana; the fleshy processes (*manikah*) on the neck and three gristles (*kikasah*) to the Gravastut; three

1. Atreya Brahmana (Martin Haug) II p. 93.
2. Manota means the deity to whom the offering is dedicated.
3. Atreya Brahmana (Martin Haug) II pp. 441-42.

other gristles and one-half of the fleshy part on the back (*vaikartta*) to the Unnetar; the other half of the fleshy part on the neck and the left lobe (*kloma*) to the slaughterer, who should present it to a Brahmana, if he himself would not happen to be a Brahmana. The head is to be given to the Subrahmanya, the skin belongs to him (the Subrahmanya), who spoke, *svah sutyam* (tomorrow at the Soma sacrifice); that part of the sacrificial animal at a Soma sacrifice which belongs to Ila (sacrificial food) is common to all the priests; only for the Hotar it is optional.

All these portions of the sacrificial animal amount to thirtysix single pieces, each of which represents the pada (foot) of a verse by which the sacrifice is carried up. The Brihati metre consists of thirty-six syllables; and the heavenly worlds are of the Brihati nature. In this way (by dividing the animal into thirtysix parts) they gain life (in this world) and the heavens, and having become established in both (this and that world) they walk there.

To those who divide the sacrificial animal in the way mentioned, it becomes the guide to heaven. But those who make the division otherwise are like scoundrels and miscreants who kill an animal merely (for gratifying their lust after flesh). This division of the sacrificial animal was invented by the Rishi (*Devabhaga*, a son of *Sruta*). When he was departing from this life, he did not entrust (the secret to anyone). But a supernatural being communicated it to *Girija*, the son of *Babhru*. Since his time men study it."

What is said by the Atreya Brahmana places two things beyond dispute. One is that the Brahmins monopolised the whole of the flesh of the sacrificial animal. Except for a paltry bit they did not even allow the sacrificer to share in it. The second is that the Brahmins themselves played the part of butchers in the slaughter of the animal. As a matter of principle the Brahmins should not eat the flesh of the animal killed at a sacrifice. The principle underlying Yajna is that man should offer himself as sacrifice to the gods. He offers an animal only to release himself from this obligation. From this it followed that the animal, being only a substitute for the man, eating the flesh of animal meant eating human flesh. This theory was very detrimental to the interest of the Brahmins who had a complete monopoly of the flesh of the animal offered for sacrifice. The Atreya Brahamana which had seen in this theory the danger of the Brahmins being deprived of the flesh of sacrificial animal takes pains to explain away the theory by a simple negation. It says[1] :

> "The man who is initiated (into the sacrificial mysteries) offers himself to all deities. Agni represents all deities and Soma represents all deities. When he (the sacrificer) offers the animal to Agni-Soma he releases himself (by being represented by the animal) from being offered to all deities.
>
> They say : " do not eat from the animal offered to Agni-Soma. Who eats from this animal, eats from human flesh ; because the sacrificer releases himself (from being sacrificed) by means of the animal". But this (precept) is not to be attended to.

Given these facts, no further evidence seems to be necessary to support the statement that the Brahmins were not merely beef-eaters but they were also butchers.

Why then did the Brahmins change front ? Let us deal with their change of front in two stages. First, why did they give up beef-eating ?

II

As has already been shown cow-killing was not legally prohibited by Asoka. Even if it had been prohibitèd, a law made by the Buddhist Emperor could never have been accepted by the Brahmins as binding upon them.

Did Manu prohibit beef-eating ? If he did, then that

1. Atreya Brahmana (Martin Haug) II p. 80.

would be binding on the Brahmins and would afford an adequate explanation of their change of front. Looking into the Manu Smriti one does find the following verses :

"V. 46. He who does not seek to cause the sufferings of bonds and death to living creatures, (but) desires the good of all (beings), obtains endless bliss.

"V. 47. He who does not injure any (creature) attains without an effort what he thinks of, what he undertakes, and what he fixes his mind on.

"V. 48. Meat can never be obtained without injury to living creatures, and injury to sentient being is detrimental to (the attainment of) heavenly bliss; let him therefore shun (the use of) meat.

"V. 49. Having well considered the (disgusting) origin of flesh and the (cruelty of) fettering and slaying corporeal beings, let him entirely abstain from eating flesh."

If these verses can be treated as containing positive injunctions they would be sufficient to explain why the Brahmins gave up meat-eating and became vegetarians. But it is impossible to treat these verses as positive injunctions, carrying the force of law. They are either exhortations or interpolations introduced after the Brahmins had become vegetarians in praise of the change. That the latter is the correct view is proved by the following verses which occur in the same chapter of the Manu Smriti.

"V. 28: The Lord of creatures (Prajapati) created this whole world to be the sustenance of the vital spirit; both the immovable and the movable creation is the food of the vital spirit.

'V. 29. What is destitute of motion is the food of those endowed with locomotion; (animals) without fangs *(are the food) of those with fangs*, those without hands of those who possess hands, and the timid of the bold,

"V. 30. The eater who daily even devours those destined to be his food, commits no sin; for the creator himself created both the eaters and those who are to be eaten (for those special purposes).

"V. 56. There is no sin in eating meat, in drinking spirituous liquor, and in carnal intercourse for that is the natural way of created beings, but abstention brings great rewards.

"V. 27. One may eat meat when it has been sprinkled with water, while mantras were recited, when Brahmans desire (one's doing it) when one is engaged (in the performance of a rite) according to the law, and when one's life is in danger.

V. 31. The consumption of meat (is befitting) for sacrifices, 'that is declared to be a rule made by the gods; but to persist (in using it) on other (occasions) is said to be a proceeding worthy of Rakshasas.

"V. 32. He who eats meat, when he honours the gods and manes, commits no sin, whether he has bought it, or himself has killed the animal or has received it as a present for others.

"V. 42. A twice-born man who, knowing the true meaning of the Veda, slays an animal for these purposes, causes both himself and the animal to enter a most blessed state.

"V. 39. Swayambhu (the self-existent) himself created animals for the sake of sacrifices; sacrifices (have been instituted) for the good of this whole (world) hence the slaughtering (of beasts) for sacrifice is not slaughtering (in the ordinary) sense of the word.

"V. 40. Herbs, trees, cattle, birds, and other animals that have been destroyed for sacrifices, receive (being reborn) higher existence."

M anu goes further and makes eating of flesh compulsory. No tə the following verse :—

"V. 35. But a man who, being duly engaged (to officiate or to dine at a sacred rite), refuses to eat meat becomes after death an animal during twentyone existences."

That Manu did not prohibit meat-eating is evident enough. That Manu Smriti did not prohibit cow-killing can also be proved from the Smriti itself. In the first place, the only references to cow in the Manu Smriti are to be found in the catalogue of rules which are made applicable by Manu to the Snataka. They are set out below :—

1. A Snataka should not eat food which a cow has smelt.[1]
2. A Snataka should not step over a rope to which a calf is tied.[2]
3. A Snataka should not urinate in a cowpan.[3]
4. A Snataka should not answer call of nature facing a cow.[4]
5. A Snataka should keep his right arm uncovered when he enters a cowpan.[5]
6. A Snataka should not interrupt a cow which is sucking her calf, nor tell anybody of it.[6]
7. A Snataka should not ride on the back of the cow.[7]
8. A Snataka should not offend the cow.[8]
9. A Snataka who is impure must not touch a cow with his hand.[9]

From these references it will be seen that Manu did not regard the cow as a sacred animal. On the other hand, he regarded it as an impure animal whose touch caused ceremonial pollution.

There are verses in Manu which show that he did not prohibit the eating of beef. In this connection, reference may be made to Chapter III. 3. It says :—

1. IV.209
2. IV.38
3. IV.45
4. IV.48
5. IV.58
6. IV.59
7. IV.70
8. IV 162
9. IV.142

"He (Snataka) who is famous (for the strict performance of) his duties and has received his heritage, the Veda from his father, shall be honoured, sitting on couch and adorned with a garland with the present of a cow (the honey-mixture)."

The question is why should Manu recommend the gift of a cow to a Snataka? Obviously, to enable him to perform Madhuparka. If that is so, it follows that Manu knew that Brahmins did eat beef and he had no objection to it.

Another reference would be to Manu's discussion of the animals whose meat is eatable and those whose meat is not. In Chapter V. 18. he says:—

The porcupine, the hedgehog, the iguana, the rhinoceros, the tortoise, and the hare they declare to be eatable, likewise those (domestic animals) that have teeth in one jaw only, excepting camels."

In this verse Manu gives general permission to eat the flesh of all domestic animals that have teeth in one jaw only. To this rule Manu makes one exception, namely, the camel. In this class of domestic animals - those that have teeth in one jaw only - falls not only the camel but also the cow. It is noteworthy that Manu does not make an exception in the case of the cow. This means that Manu had no objection to the eating of the cow's flesh.

Manu did not make the killing of the cow an offence. Manu divides sins into two classes (i) mortal sins and (ii) minor sins. Among the mortal sins Manu includes:

"XI. 55. Killing a Brahmana, drinking (the spirituos liquor called Sura) stealing the (gold of the Brahmana) adultery with a Guru's wife, and associating with such offenders."

Among minor sins Manu includes:

"XI. 60. Killing the cow, sacrificing for those unworthy to sacrifice, adultery, setting oneself, casting off one's teacher, mother, father or son, giving up the (daily) study of the Veda and neglecting the (sacred domestic) fire,"

From this it will be clear that according to Manu cow-killing was only a minor sin. It was reprehensible only if the cow was killed without good and sufficient reason. Even if it was otherwise, it was not heinous or inexplicable. The same was the attitude of Yajnavalkya[1].

All this proves that for generations the Brahmins had been eating beef. Why did they give up beef-eating? Why did they, as an extreme step, give up meat eating altogether and become vegetarians ? It is two revolutions rolled into one. As has been shown it has not been done as a result of the preachings of Manu, their Divine Law-maker. The revolution has taken place in spite of Manu and contrary to his directions. What made the Brahmins take this step ? Was philosophy responsible for it ? Or was it dictated by strategy ?

Two explanations are offered. One explanation is that this deification of the cow was a manifestation of the Advaita philosophy that one supreme entity pervaded the whole universe, that on that account all life human as well as animal was sacred. This explanation is obviously unsatisfactory. In the first place, it does not fit in with facts. The Vedanta Sutra which proclaims the doctrine of oneness of life does not prohibit the killing of animals for sacrificial purposes as is evident from II.1.28. In the second place, if the transformation was due to the desire to realize the ideal of Advaita then there is no reason why it should have stopped with the cow. It should have extended to all other animals.

Another explanation[2] more ingenious than the first, is that this transformation in the life of the Brahmin was due to the rise of the doctrine of the Transmigration of the Soul. Even this explanation does not fit in with facts. The Brahadranyaka Upanishad upholds the doctrine of transmigration (vi. 2) and yet recommends that if a man desires to have a learned son born to him he should prepare a mass of the flesh of the bull or ox or of other flesh with rice and ghee. Again, how is it that this doctrine which is propounded in the Upanishads did not have any effect on the Brahmins

1. Yaj. III. 227 and III 234.
2. Kane's Dharma Shastra II. Part II. P 776.

up to the time of the Manu Smriti, a period of at least 400 years. Obviously, this explanation is no explanation. Thirdly, if Brahmins became vegetarians by reason of the doctrine of transmigration of the soul how is it, it did not make the non-Brahmins take to vegetarianism?

To my mind, it was strategy which made the Brahmins give up beef-eating and start worshipping the cow. The clue to the worship of the cow is to be found in the struggle between Buddhism and Brahmanism and the means adopted by Brahmanism to establish its supremacy over Buddhism. The strife between Buddhism and Brahmanism is a crucial fact in Indian history. Without the realisation of this fact, it is impossible to explain some of the features of Hinduism. Unfortunately students of Indian history have entirely missed the importance of this strife. They knew there was Brahmanism. But they seem to be entirely unaware of the struggle for supremacy in which these creeds were engaged and that their struggle which extended for 400 years has left some indelible marks on religion, society and politics of India.

This is not the place for describing the full story of the struggle. All one can do is to mention a few salient points. Buddhism was at one time the religion of the majority of the people of India. It continued to be the religion of the masses for hundreds of years. It attacked Brahmanism on all sides as no religion had done before. Brahmanism was on the wane and if not on the wane, it was certainly on the defensive. As a result of the spread of Buddhism, the Brahmins had lost all power and prestige at the Royal Court and among the people. They were smarting under the defeat they had suffered at the hands of Buddhism and were making all possible efforts to regain their power and prestige. Buddhism had made so deep an impression on the minds of the masses and had taken such a hold of them that it was absolutely impossible for the Brahmins to fight the Buddhists except by accepting their ways and means and practising the Buddhist creed in its extreme form. After the death of Buddha his followers started setting up the images of the Buddha and building stupas. The Brahmins followed it. They, in their turn, built temples and installed in them images of Shiva, Vishnu and Ram and Krishna etc., – all with the object of drawing away the crowd that was attracted by the image worship of Buddha. That is how temples and images which had no place in Brahmanism came into Hinduism. The Buddhists rejected the Brahmanic religion which consisted of Yajna and animal sacrifice, particularly of the cow. The objection to the sacrifice of the cow had taken a strong hold of the minds of the masses especially as they were an agricultural population and the cow was a very useful animal. The Brahmins in all probability had come to be hated as the killer of cows in the same way as the guest had come to be hated as *Gognha,* the killer of the cow by the householder, because whenever he came a cow had to be killed in his honour. That being the case, the Brahmins could do nothing to improve their position against the Buddhists except by giving up the Yajna as a form of worship and the sacrifice of the cow.

That the object of the Brahmins in giving up beef-eating was to snatch away from the Buddhist Bikhus the supremacy they had acquired is evidenced by the adoption of vegetarianism by Brahmins. Why did the Brahmin become vegetarian ? The answer is that without becoming vegetarian the Brahmins could have recovered the ground they had lost in its revival namely, Buddhism. In this connection it must be remembered that there was one aspect in which Brahmanism suffered in public esteem as compared to Buddhism. That was the practice of animal sacrifice which was the essence of Brahmanism and to which Buddhism was deadly opposed. That in an agricultural population there should be respect for Buddhism and revulsion against Brahmanism which involved slaughter of animals including cows and bullocks is only natural. What could the Brahmins do to recover the lost ground? To go one better than the Buddhist Bhikshus - not only to give up meat-eating but to become vegetarians - which they did. That this was the object of the Brahmins in becoming vegetarians can be proved in various ways.

If the Brahmins had acted from conviction that animal sacrifice was bad, all that was necessary for them to do was to give up killing animals for sacrifice. It was unnecessary for them to be vegetarians. That they did go in for vegetarianism makes it obvious that their motive was far-reaching.

Secondly, it was unnecessary for them to become vegetarians. For the Buddhist Bhikshus were not vegetarians. This statement might surprise many people owing to the popular belief that the connection between Ahimsa and Buddhism was immediate and essential. It is generally believed that the Buddhist Bhikshus eschewed animal food. This is an error. The fact is that the Buddhist Bhikshus were permitted to eat three kinds of flesh that were deemed pure. Later on they were extended to five classes. Yuan Chwang the Chinese traveller was aware of this and spoke of the pure kinds of flesh as *San-Ching*. The origin of this practice among the Bhikshus is explained by Mr Thomas Walters. According to the story told by him[1]—

> "In the time of Buddha there was in Vaisali a wealthy general named Siha who was a convert to Buddhism. He became a liberal supporter of the Brethren and kept them constantly supplied with good flesh- food. When it was noticed abroad that the Bhikshus were in the habit of eating such food specially provided for them, the Tirthikas made the practice a matter of angry reproach. Then the abstemious ascetic Brethren, learning this, reported the circumstances to the Master, who thereupon called the Brethren together. When they assembled, he announced to them the law that they were not to eat the flesh of any animal which they had seen put to death for them, or about which they had been told that it had been slain for them. But he permitted to the Brethren as 'pure' (that is, lawful) food the flesh of animals the slaughter of which had not been seen by the Bhikshus, not heard of by them, and not suspected by them to have been on their account. In the Pali and *Ssu-fen* Vinaya it was after a breakfast given by Siha to the Buddha and some of the Brethren, for which the carcase of a large ox was procured that the Nirgranthas reviled the Bhikshus and Buddha instituted this new rule declaring fish and flesh 'pure' in the three conditions. The

1. Yuan Chwang (1904) Vol. I. p. 55.

> animal food now permitted to the Bhikshus came to be known as the 'three pures' or 'three pure kinds of flesh', and it was tersely described as 'unseen, unheard, unsuspected', or as the Chinese translations sometimes have it 'not seen, not heard nor suspected to be on my account'. Then two more kinds of animal food were declared "lawful for the Brethren viz., the flesh of animals which had died a natural death, and that of animals which had been killed by a bird of prey or other savage creature. So there came to be five classes or descriptions of flesh which the professed Buddhist was at liberty to use as food. Then the 'unseen, unheard, unsuspected' came to be treated as one class, and this together with the 'natural death' and 'bird killed' made a *San-ching*."

As the Buddhist Bhikshus did eat meat the Brahmins had no reason to give it up. Why then did the Brahmins give up meat-eating and become vegetarians? It was because they did not want to put themselves merely on the same footing in the eyes of the public as the Buddhist Bhikshus.

The giving up of the Yajna system and abandonment of the sacrifice of the cow could have had only a limited effect. At the most it would have put the Brahmins on the same footing as the Buddhists. The same would have been the case if they had followed the rules observed by the Buddhist Bhikshus in the matter of meat-eating. It could not have given the Brahmins the means of achieving supremacy over the Buddhists which was their ambition. They wanted to oust the Buddhists from the place of honour and respect which they had acquired in the minds of the masses by their opposition to the killing of the cow for sacrificial purposes. To achieve their purpose the Brahmins had to adopt the usual tactics of a wreckless adventurer. It is to beat extremism by extremism. It is the strategy which all rightists use to overcome the leftists. The only way to beat the Buddhists was to go a step further and be vegetarians.

There is another reason which can be relied upon to support the thesis that the Brahmins started cow-worship, gave up beef-eating and became vegetarians in order to vanquish Buddhism. It is the date when cow-killing became a mortal sin. It is well-known that cow-killing was not made an offence by Asoka. Many people expect him to have come forward to prohibit the killing of the cow. Prof. Vincent Smith regards it as surprising. But there is nothing surprising in it.

Buddhism was against animal sacrifice in general. It had no particular affection for the cow. Asoka had therefore no particular reason to make a law to save the cow. What is more astonishing is the fact that cow-killing was made a *Mahapataka*, a mortal sin or a capital offence by the Gupta Kings who were champions of Hinduism which recognised and sanctioned the killing of the cow for sacrificial purposes. As pointed out by Mr. D.R. Bhandarkar[1] —

> "We have got the incontrovertible evidence of inscriptions to show that early in the 5th century A. D. killing a cow was looked upon as an offence of the deepest turpitude, turpitude as deep as that involved in murdering a Brahman. We have thus a copper-plate inscription dated 465 A.D. and referring itself to the reign of Skandagupta of the Imperial Gupta dynasty. It registers a grant and ends with a verse saying : 'Whosoever will transgress this grant that has been assigned (shall become as guilty as) the slayer of a cow, the slayer of a spiritual preceptor (or) the slayer of a Brahman. A still earlier record placing *go-hatya* on the same footing as *brahma hatya* is that of Chandragupta II, grandfather of Skandagupta just mentioned. It bears the Gupta date 93, which is equivalent to 412 A.D. It is engraved on the railing which surrounds the celebrated Buddhist stupa at Sanchi, in Central India. This also speaks of a benefaction made by an officer of Chadragupta and ends as follows : ... . "Whosoever shall interfere with this arrangement - he shall become invested with (the guilt of) the slaughter

1. Some Aspects of Ancient Indian Culture. (1940). pp. 78-79.

of a cow or of a Brahman, and with (the guilt of) the five *anantarya.*" Here the object of this statement is to threaten the resumer of the grant, be he a Brahminist or a Buddhist, with the sins regarded as mortal by each community. The *anantaryas* are the five *mahapatakas* according to Buddhist theology. They are : matricide, patricide, killing an Arhat, shedding the blood of a Buddha, and causing a split among the priesthood. The *mahapatakas* with which a Brahminist is here threatened are only two : viz., the killing of a cow and the murdering of a Brahman. The latter is obviously a *mahapataka* as it is mentioned as such in all the Smritis, but the former has been specified only an *upapataka* by Apastamba, Manu, Yajnavalkya and so forth. But the very fact that it is here associated with *brahma-hatya* and both have been put on a par with the *anantaryas* of the Buddhists shows that in the beginning of the fifth century A.D., it was raised to the category of *mahapatakas.* Thus *go-hatya* must have come to be considered a *mahapataka* at least one century earlier, i.e., about the commencement of the fourth century A.D."

The question is why should a Hindu king have come forward to make a law against cow-killing, that is to say, against the Laws of Manu? The answer is that the Brahmins had to suspend or abrogate a requirement of their Vedic religion in order to overcome the supremacy of the Buddhist Bhikshus. If the analysis is correct then it is obvious that the worship of the cow is the result of the struggle between Buddhism and Brahminism. It was a means adopted by the Brahmins to regain their lost position.

CHAPTER XIV

Why should Beef-eating make Broken Men Untouchables?

The stoppage of beef-eating by the Brahmins and the non-Brahmins and the continued use thereof by the Broken Men had produced a situation which was different from the old. This difference lay in the fact that while in the old situation everybody ate beef, in the new situation one section did not and another did. The difference was a glaring difference. Everybody could see it. It divided society as nothing else did before. All the same, this difference need not have given rise to such extreme division of society as is marked by Untouchability. It could have remained a social difference. There are many cases where different sections of the community differ in their foods. What one likes the other dislikes and yet this difference does not create a bar between the two.

There must therefore be some special reason why in India the difference between the Settled Community and the Broken Men in the matter of beef-eating created a bar between the two. What can that be? The answer is that if beef-eating had remained a secular affair—a mere matter of individual taste—such a bar between those who ate beef and those who did not would not have arisen. Unfortunately beef-eating, instead of being treated as a purely secular matter, was made a matter of religion. This happened because the Brahmins made the cow a sacred animal. This made beef-eating a sacrilege. The Broken Men being guilty of sacrilege necessarily became beyond the pale of Society.

The answer may not be quite clear to those who have no idea of the scope and function of religion in the life of the society. They may ask: Why should religion make such a difference? It will be clear if the following points regarding the scope and function of religion are borne in mind.

To begin with the definition[1] of religion. There is one

[1] This definition of religion is by Prof. E'nvile Durkhiem, See his 'The Elementary Forms of the Religious Life' p. 47. For the discussion that follows I have drawn upon the same authority.

universal feature which characterises all religions. This feature lies in religion being a unified system of beliefs and practices which (1) relate to sacred things and (2) which unite into one single community all those who adhere to them. To put it slightly differently, there are two elements in every religion. One is that religion is inseparable from sacred things. The other is that religion is a collective thing inseparable from society.

The first element in religion presupposes a classification of all things, real and ideal, which are the subject-matter of man's thought, into two distinct classes which are generally designated by two distinct terms the *sacred* and the *profane*, popularly spoken of as secular.

This defines the scope of religion. For understanding the function of religion the following points regarding things sacred should be noted :

The first thing to note is that things sacred are not merely higher than or superior in dignity and status to those that are profane. They are just different. The sacred and the profane do not belong to the same class. There is a complete dichotomy between the two. As Prof. Durkhiem observes[1] :—

> "The traditional opposition of good and bad is nothing beside this ; for the good and the bad are only two opposed species of the same class, namely, morals, just as sickness and health are two different aspects of the same order of facts, life, while the sacred and the profane have always and everywhere been conceived by the human mind as two distinct classes, as two worlds between which there is nothing in common."

The curious may want to know what has led men to see in this world this dichotomy between the sacred and profane. We must however refuse to enter into this discussion as it is unnecessary for the immediate purpose we have in mind.[2]

1. Prof. Durkhiem's 'The Elementary Forms of the Religious Life.' p. 38.
2. The curious may refer to page 317 of the above book.

Confining ourselves to the issue the next thing to note is that the circle of sacred objects is not fixed. Its extent varies infinitely from religion to religion. Gods and spirits are not the only sacred things. A rock, a tree, an animal, a spring, a pebble, a piece of wood, a house, in a word anything can be sacred.

Things sacred are always associated with interdictions otherwise called *taboos*. To quote Prof. Durkhiem[1] again:

> "Sacred things are those which the interdictions protect and isolate; profane things, those to which these interdictions are applied and which must remain at a distance from the first."

Religious interdicts take multiple forms. Most important of these is the interdiction on contact. The interdiction on contact rests upon the principle that the profane should never touch the sacred. Contact may be established in a variety of ways other than touch. A look is a means of contact. That is why the sight of sacred things is forbidden to the profane in certain cases. For instance, women are not allowed to see certain things which are regarded as sacred. The word (i.e., the breath which forms part of man and which spreads outside him) is another means of contact. That is why the profane is forbidden to address the sacred things or to utter them. For instance, the Veda must be uttered only by the Brahmin and not by the Shudra. An exceptionally intimate contact is the one resulting from the absorption of food. Hence comes the interdiction against eating the sacred animals or vegetables.

The interdictions relating to the sacred are not open to discussion. They are beyond discussion and must be accepted without question. The sacred is 'untouchable' in the sense that it is beyond the pale of debate. All that one can do is to respect and obey.

Lastly the interdictions relating to the sacred are binding on all. They are not maxims. They are injunctions. They are obligatory but not in the ordinary sense of the word.

1. 'The Elementary Forms of the Religions Life' p. 41. Interdictions which come from religion must be distinguished from those which proceed from magic. For a discussion of this subject see Ibid. p. 300.

They partake of the nature of a categorical imperative. Their breach is more than a crime. It is a sacrilege.

The above summary should be enough for an understanding of the scope and function of religion. It is unnecessary to enlarge upon the subject further. The analysis of the working of the laws of the sacred which is the core of religion should enable any one to see that my answer to the question why beef-eating should make the Broken Men untouchables is the correct one. All that is necessary to reach the answer I have proposed is to read the analysis of the working of the laws of the sacred with the cow as the sacred object. It will be found that Untouchability is the result of the breach of the interdiction against the eating of the sacred animal, namely, the cow.

As has been said, the Brahmins made the cow a sacred animal. They did not stop to make a difference between a living cow and a dead cow. The cow was sacred, living or dead. Beef-eating was not merely a crime. If it was only a crime it would have involved nothing more than punishment. Beef-eating was made a sacrilege. Anyone who treated the cow as profane was guilty of sin and unfit for association. The Broken Men who continued to eat beef became guilty of sacrilege.

Once the cow became sacred and the Broken Men continued to eat beef, there was no other fate left for the Broken Men except to be treated unfit for association, i.e., as Untouchables.

Before closing the subject it may be desirable to dispose of possible objections to the thesis. Two such objections to the thesis appear obvious. One is what evidence is there that the Broken Men did eat the flesh of the dead cow. The second is why did they not give up beef-eating when the Brahmins and the non-Brahmins abandoned it. These questions have an important bearing upon the theory of the origin of untouchability advanced in this book and must therefore be dealt with.

The first question is relevant as well as crucial. If the Broken Men were eating beef from the very beginning, then obviously the theory cannot stand. For, if they were eating beef from the very beginning and nonetheless were not treated as Untouchables, to say that the Broken Men became Untouchables because of beef-eating would be illogical if not senseless. The second question is relevant, if not crucial. If the Brahmins gave up beef-eating and the non-Brahmins imitated them why did the Broken Men not do the same? If the law made the killing of the cow a capital sin because the cow became a sacred animal to the Brahmins and non-Brahmins, why were the Broken Men not stopped from eating beef? If they had been stopped from eating beef there would have been no Untouchability.

The answer to the first question is that even during the period when beef-eating was common to both the Settled Tribesmen and the Broken Men a system had grown up whereby the Settled Community ate fresh beef, while the Broken Men ate the flesh of the dead cow. We have no positive evidence to show that members of the Settled Community never ate the flesh of the dead cow. But we have negative evidence which shows that the dead cow had become an exclusive possession and perquisite of the Broken Men. The evidence consists of facts which relate to the Mahars of the Maharashtra to whom reference has already been made. As has already been pointed out, the Mahars of the Maharashtra claim the right to take the dead animal. This right they claim against every Hindu in the village. This means that no Hindu can eat the flesh of his own animal when it dies. He has to surrender it to the Mahar. This is merely another way of stating that when eating beef was a common practice the Mahars ate dead beef and the Hindus ate fresh beef. The only questions that arise are : Whether what is true of the present is true of the ancient past ? Can this fact which is true of the Maharashtra be taken as typical of the arrangement between the Settled Tribes and the Broken Men throughout India ?

In this connection reference may be made to the tradition current among the Mahars according to which they claim that they were given 52 rights against the Hindu villagers by the Muslim King of Bedar. Assuming that they were given by the King of Bedar, the King obviously did not create them for the first time. They must have been in existence from the ancient past. What the King did was merely to confirm them. This means that the practice of the Broken Men eating dead meat and the Settled Tribes eating fresh meat must have grown in the ancient past. That such an arrangement should grow up is certainly most natural. The Settled Community was a wealthy community with agricultural and cattle as means of livelihood. The Broken Men were a community of paupers with no means of livelihood and entirely dependent upon the Settled Community. The principal item of food for both was beef. It was possible for the Settled Community to kill an animal for food because it was possessed of cattle. The Broken Men could not for they had none. Would it be unnatural in these circumstances for the Settled Community to have agreed to give to the Broken Men its dead animals as part of their wages of watch and ward ? Surely not. It can therefore be taken for granted that in the ancient past when both the Settled Community and Broken Men did eat beef the former ate fresh beef and the latter of the dead cow and that this system represented a universal state of affairs thoughout India and was not confined to the Maharashtra

This disposes of the first objection. To turn to the second objection. The law made by the Gupta Emperors was intended to prevent those who killed cows. It did not apply to the Broken Men. For they did not kill the cow. They only ate the dead cow. Their conduct did not contravene the law against cow-killing. The practice of eating the flesh of the dead cow therefore was allowed to continue. Nor did their conduct contravene the doctrine of Ahimsa assuming that it had anything to do with the abandonment of beef-eating by the Brahmins and the non-raBhmins. Killing the cow was Himsa. But eating the dead cow was not. The Broken Men had therefore no cause for feeling qualms of conscience in continuing to eat the dead cow. Neither the law nor the doctrine of Himsa could interdict what they were doing, for what they were doing was neither contrary to law nor to the doctrine.

As to why they did not imitate the Brahmins and the non-Brahmins the answer is twofold. In the first place, imitation was too costly. They could not afford it. The flesh of the dead cow was their principal sustenance. Without it they would starve. In the second place, carrying the dead cow had become an obligation[1] though originally it was a privilege As they could not escape carrying the dead cow they did not mind using the flesh as food in the manner in which they were doing previously.

The objections therefore do not invalidate the thesis in any way.

---

1. Owing to the reform movement among the Mahars the position has become just the reverse. The Mahars refuse to take the dead animal while the Hindu villagers force them to take it.

PART VI

Untouchability and the Date of its Birth

Chapter XV. The Impure and The Untouchables.

Chapter XVI. When did Broken Men become Untouchables?

CHAPTER XV

The Impure and The Untouchables

I

When did Untouchability come into existence? The orthodox Hindus insist that it is very ancient in its origin. In support of their contention reliance is placed on the fact that the observance of Untouchability is enjoined not merely by the Smritis which are of a later date but it is also enjoined by the Dharma Sutras which are much earlier and which, according to certain authors, date some centuries before B.C.

In a study devoted to exploring the origin of Untouchability the question one must begin with is: Is Untouchability as old as is suggested to be?

For an answer to this question one has to examine the Dharma Sutras in order to ascertain what they mean when they refer to Untouchability and to the Untouchables. Do they mean by Untouchability what we understand by it to-day? Do the class, to which they refer, Untouchables in the sense in which we use the term Untouchables to-day?

To begin with the first question. An examination of the Dharma Sutras no doubt shows that they speak of a class whom they call Asprashya. There is also no doubt that the term Asprashya does mean Untouchable. The question however remains whether the Asprashya of the Dharma Sutras are the same as the Asprashya of modern India. This question becomes important when it is realized that the Dharma Sutras also use a variety of other terms such as Antya, Antyaja, Antyavasin and Bahya. These terms are also used by the later Smritis. It might be well to have some idea of the use of these terms by the different Sutras and Smritis. The following table is intended to serve that purpose :—

I. Asprashya

Dharma Sutra	Smriti
1. Vishnu V. 104.	1. Katyayana verses 433, 783.

II. Antya

Dharma Sutras	Smriti
1. Vasishta. (16-30) 2. Apastambha (III.I)	1. Manu IV. 79; VIII. 68 2. Yajnavalkya I. 148. 197. 3. Atri 25. 4. Likhita 92.

III. Bahya

Dharma Sutra	Smriti
1. Apastambha 1.2.39.18 2. Vishnu 16. 14	1. Manu 28. 2. Narada I.155.

IV. Antyavasin

Dharma Sutra	Smriti
1. Gautama XXXI; XXIII 32 2. Vasishta XVIII. 3	1. Manu IV. 79; X.39 2. Shanti Parvan of the Mahabharatha 141; 29-32 3. Madhyamangiras (quoted in Mitakshara on Yaj. 3.280.

V. Antyaja

Dharma Sutra	Smriti
1. Vishnu 36.7	1. Manu IV. 61; VIII. 279
	2. Yajnavalkya 12.73
	3. Brihadyama Smriti (quoted by Mitakshara on Yajnavalkya III. 260)
	4. Atri. 199
	5. Veda Vyas 1. 12. 13.

II

The next question is whether the classes indicated by the terms Antya, Antyaja, Antyavasin and Bahya are the same as those indicated by the term Asprashya which etymologically means an Untouchable. In other words are they only different names for the same class of people ?

It is an unfortunate fact that the Dharma Sutras do not enable us to answer this question. The term *Asprashya* occurs in two places (in one Sutra and one Smriti). But not one gives an enumeration of the classes included in it. The same is the case with the term *Antya*. Although the word *Antya* occurs in six places (in two Sutras and four Smritis) not one enumerates who they are. Similarly, the word *Bahya* occurs in four places (in two Sutras and two Smritis), but none of them mentions what communities are included under this term. The only exception is with regard to the terms Antyavasin and Antyajas. Here again no Dharma Sutra enumerates them. But there is an enumeration of them in the Smritis. The enumeration of the Antyavasin occurs in the Smriti known as Madhyamangiras and that of the Antyajas in the Atri Smriti and Veda Vyas Smriti. Who they are, will be apparent from the following table :--

ANTYAVASIN	ANTYAJA	
Madhyamangiras.	Atri	Veda Vyas
1. **Chandala**.	1. Nata.	1. **Chandala.**
2. **Shvapaka**.	2. Meda.	2. **Shvapaka**.
3. Kshatta.	3. Bhilla.	3. Nata.
4. Suta.	4. **Rajaka**,	4. Meda.
5. Vaidehika.	5. **Charmkar.**	5. Bhilla.
6. Magadha	6. Buruda.	6. **Rajaka**
7. Ayogava.	7. Kayavarta.	7. **Charmkar**.
		8. Virat.
		9. Dasa.
		10. Bhatt.
		11. Kolika.
		12. Pushkar.

From this table it is quite clear that there is neither precision nor agreement with regard to the use of the terms Antyavasin and Antyaja. For instance Chandala and Shvapak fall in both the categories Antyavasin and Antyaja according to Madhyamangiras and Veda Vyas. But when one compares Madhyamangiras with Atri they fall in different categories. The same is true with regard to the term Antyaja. For example while (1) Chandala and (2) Shvapaka are Antyajas according to Veda Vyas, according to Atri they are not

Again according to Atri (1) Buruda and (2) Kayavarta are Antyajas while according to Veda Vyas they are not. Again (1) Virat (2) Dasa (3) Bhatt (4) Kolika and (5) Pushkar are Antyaja according to Veda Vyas but according to Atri they are not.

To sum up the position reached so far : neither the Dharma Sutras nor the Smritis help us to ascertain who were included in the category of Asprashya. Equally useless are the Dharma Sutras and the Smritis to enable us to ascertain whether the classes spoken of as Antyavasin, Antyaja and Bahya were the same as Asprashya. Is there any other way of ascertaining whether any of these formed into the category of Asprashya or Untouchables? It would be better to collect together whatever information is available about each of these classes.

What about the Bahyas? Who are they? What are they? Are they Untouchables? They are mentioned by Manu. To understand their position, it is necessary to refer to Manu's scheme of social classification. Manu divides the people into various categories. He first[1] makes a broad division between (1) Vaidikas and (2) Dasyus. He then proceeds to divide the Vaidikas into four sub-divisions : (1) Those inside Chaturvarnya (2) Those outside Chaturvarnya (3) Vratya and (4) Patitas or outcastes.

Whether a person was inside Chaturvarnya or outside. was a question to be determined by the Varna of the parents. If he was born of the parents of the same Varnas, he was inside the Chaturvarnya. If, on the other hand, he was born of parents of different Varnas i.e. he was the progeny of mixed marriages or what Manu calls *Varna Samkara*, then he was outside the Chaturvarnya. Those outside Chaturvarnya are further sub-divided by Manu into two classes (1) Anulomas and (2) Pratilomas. Anulomas[2] were those whose fathers were of a higher Varna and mothers of a lower Varna. Pratilomas, on the other hand, were those whose fathers were of a lower Varna and the mothers of a higher Varna. Though both the Anulomas and Pratilomas were alike for the reason that they were outside the Chaturvarnya, Manu proceeds to make a distinction between them. The Anulomas,

1. See Manu 1. 45. 2. See Manu 1. 45.

he calls Varna Bahya or shortly *Bahyas*, while Pratilomas he calls *Hinas*. The Hinas are lower than the Bahyas. But neither the Bahyas nor the Hinas does Manu regard as Untouchables.

Antya as a class is mentioned in Manu IV.79. Manu however does not enumerate them. Medhatithi in his commentary suggests that Antya means Mlecha, such as Meda etc. Buhler translates Antya as a low-caste man.

There is thus nothing to indicate that the Antyas were Untouchables. In all probability, it is the name given to those people who were living in the outskirts or *end* (Anta) of the village. The reason why they came to be regarded as low is to be found in the story narrated in the Brihadranyaka Upanishad (I.3) to which reference is made by Mr. Kane.[1] The story is that—

> "Gods and Asuras had a strike and the gods thought that they might rise superior to the Asuras by the Udgithana. In this occurs the passage 'this devata (Prana) throwing aside the sin that was death to these devatas (vak etc.) sent it to ends of these devatas there ; therefore one should not go to the people outside the Aryan pale nor to *disam anta* (the ends of the quarters) thinking 'otherwise I may fall in with papmani i.e., death".

The meaning of Antya turns on the connotation of the phrase 'disam Anta' which occurs in the passage quoted above. If the phrase 'ends of the quarters' can be translated as meaning the end of the periphery of the village, without its being called a far-fetched translation, we have here an explanation of what Antya originally meant. It does not suggest that the Antyas were Untouchables. It only meant that they were living on the outskirts of the village.

As to the Antyajas, what we know about them is enough to refute the view that they were Untouchables. Attention may be drawn to the following facts[2] :

In the Shanti Parvan (109.9) of the Mahabharat there

1. History of Dharma Shastra II. Part I. p. 167.

2. Kane—History of Dharma Shastra. Vol. II. part I. p. 70.

is a refernce to Antyajas who are spoken of as Soldiers in the Army. According to Sarasvativilasa, Pitamaha speaks of the seven castes of Rajakas included in the term Antyaja as Prakritis. That Prakritis mean trade guilds such as of washermen and others is quite clear from the Sangamner Plate of Bhillama II dated Saka 922 which records the grant of a village to eighteen Prakritis. Viramitrodya says that Srenis mean the eighteen castes such as the Rajaka etc., which-are collectively called Antyajas. In view of these facts how could the Antyajas be said to have been regarded as the Untouchables ?

Coming to the Antyavasin, who were they? Were they Untouchables ? The term Antyavasin has been used in two different senses. In one sense it was applied to a Brahmachari living in the house of the Guru during his term of studentship. A Brahmachari was referred to as Antyavasin.[1] It probably meant one who was served last. Whatever the reason for calling a Brahmachari Antyavasin it is beyond dispute that the word in that connection could not connote Untouchability. How could it when only Brahmins, Kshatriyas and Vaishyas could become Brahmacharis. In another sense they refer to a body of people. But even in this sense it is doubtful if it means Untouchables.

According to Vas.Dh.Sutra (18.3) they are the offspring of a Sudra father and Vaishya mother. But according to Manu (V.39) they are the offspring of a Chandala father and a Nishad mother. As to the class to which they belong the Mitakshara says they are a sub-group of the Antyajas which means that the Antyavasin were not different from the Antyajas. What is therefore true of the Antyajas may also be taken as true of the Antyavasin.

III

Stopping here to take stock of the situation as it emerges from such information as we have regarding the social condition of the people called Antyavasin, Antya, Antyaja, as is available from ancient literature, obviously it is not open to say that these classes were Untouchables in the modern sense of the term. However, for the satisfaction of those who may still have some doubt, the matter may be further examined

1. **Amarkosh II Kanda Brahmabarga Verse II.**

from another point of view. Granting that they were described as Asprashya we may proceed to inquire as to what was the connotation of the term in the days of the Dharma Sutras.

For this purpose we must ascertain the rules of atonement prescribed by the Shastras. From the study of these rules we will be able to see whether the term Asprashya had the same connotation in the times of the Dharma Sutras as it has now.

Let us take the case of the Chandalas as an illustration of the class called Asprashya. In the first place, it should be remembered that the word Chandala does not denote one single homogeneous class of people. It is one word for many classes of people, all different from one another. There are altogether five different classes of Chandalas who are referred to in the Shastras. They are (i) the offspring of a Shudra father and a Brahmin mother;[1] (ii) the offspring of an unmarried woman[2] (iii) the offspring of union with a sagotra woman[3] (iv) the offspring of a person who after becoming an ascetic turns back to the householder's life[4] and (v) the offspring of a barber father and a Brahmin mother[5].

It is difficult to say which Chandala calls for purification. We shall assume that purification is necessary in the case of all the Chandalas. What is the rule of purification prescribed by the Shastras ?

Gautama in his Dharma Sutra (Chapter XIV, Verse 30) also refers to it in the following terms:—

> "On touching an outcaste, a Chandala, a woman impure on account of her confinement, a woman in her courses, or a corpse and on touching persons who have touched them, he shall purify himself by bathing dressed in his clothes."

Below is the text of the rule given by the Vasishta Dharma Sutra (Chapter IV, Verse 37):—

1. According to all Dharma Sutras and Smritis including Manu Smriti.

2.3. According to Veda Vyas Smriti (1.-9?0)

4. According to Yama quoted in Parasura Madhavya.

5. Anusasan Parva (29-17). He is also called Matanga.

"When he has touched a sacrificial post, a pyre, a burial ground, a menstruating or a lately confined woman, impure men or Chandalas and so forth, he shall bathe, submerging both his body and his head."

Baudhayana agrees with Vasishta for he too in his Dharma Sutra (Prasna I, Adhyaya 5, Khanda 6, Verse 5) says:

"On touching a tree standing on a sacred spot, a funeral pyre, a sacrificial post, a Chandala or a person who sells the Veda, a Brahmin shall bathe dressed in his clothes."

The following are the rules contained in Manu:—

V.85: When he (the Brahmin) has touched a Chandala, a menstruating woman, an outcaste, a woman in childbed, a corpse, or one who has touched a (corpse), he becomes pure by bathing.

V.131: Manu has declared that the flesh of an animal killed by dogs is pure, likewise (that) of a (beast) slain by carnivorous (animals) or by men of low caste (Dasya) such as Chandalas.

V.143: He who, while carrying anything in any manner, is touched by an impure (person or thing), shall become pure, if he performs an ablution, without pulling down that object.

From these texts drawn from the Dharma Sutras as well as Manu, the following points are clear :--

(1) That the pollution by the touch of the Chandala was observed by the Brahmin only.

(2) That the pollution was probably observed on ceremonial occasions only.

IV

If these conclusions are right then this is a case of Impurity as distinguished from Untouchability. The distinction between the Impure and the Untouchable is very clear. The

Untouchable pollutes all while the Impure pollutes only the Brahmin. The touch of the Impure causes pollution only on a ceremonial occasion. The touch of the Untouchable causes pollution at all times.

There is another argument to which so far no reference has been made which completely disproves the theory that the communities mentioned in the Dharma Sutras were Untouchables. That argument emerges out of a comparison of the list of communities given in the Order-in-Council (which is reproduced in Chapter II) with the list given in this chapter prepared from the Smritis. What does the comparison show ? As anyone can see, it shows :—

Firstly : The maximum number of communities mentioned in the Smritis is only 12, while the number of communities mentioned in the Order-in-Council comes to 429.

Secondly : There are communities which find a place in the Order-in-Council but which do not find a place in the Smritis.[1] Out of the total of 429 there are nearly 427 which are unknown to the Smritis.

Thirdly : There are communities mentioned in the Smritis which do not find a place in the Order-in-Council at all.

Fourthly : There is only one community which finds a place in both. It is the Charmakar community.[2]

Those who do not admit that the Impure are different from the Untouchables do not seem to be aware of these facts. But they will have to reckon with them. These facts are so significant and so telling that they cannot but force the conclusion that the two are different.

Take the first fact. It raises a very important question.

1. Out of the 429 communities mentioned in the Order-in-Council, there are only 3 which are to be found in the list given by the Smritis.

2. There are also two other communities mentioned in both lists (1) Nata and (2) Rajaka. But according to the Order-in-Council they are Untouchables in some parts of the country only. The Chamar is Untouchable throughout India.

If the two lists refer to one and the same class of people, why do they differ and differ so widely? How is it that the communities mentioned in the Shastras do not appear in the list given in the Order-in-Council? Contrarywise, how is it that the communities mentioned in the Order-in-Council are not to be found in the list given by the Shastras? This is the first difficulty we have to face.

On the assumption that they refer to the same class of people, the question assumes a serious character. If they refer to the same class of people then obviously Untouchability which was originally confined to 12 communities came to be extended to 429 communities ! What has led to this vast extension of the Empire of Untouchability? If these 429 communities belong to the same class as the 12 mentioned by the Shastras why none of the Shastras mention them? It cannot be that none of the 429 communities were not in existence at the time when the Shastras were written. If all of them were not in existence at least some of them must have been. Why even such as did exist find no mention ?

On the footing that both the lists belong to the same class of people, it is difficult to give any satisfactory answer to these questions. If, on the other hand, it is assumed that these lists refer to two different classes of people, all these questions disappear. The two lists are different because the list contained in the Shastras is a list of the Impure and the list contained in the Order-in-Council is a list of the Untouchables. This is the reason why the two lists differ. The divergence in the two lists merely emhasizes what has been urged on other grounds, namely, that the classes mentioned in Shastras are only Impure and it is a mistake to confound them with the Untouchables of the present day.

Now turn to the second. If the Impure are the same as the Untouchables, why is it as many as 427 out 429 should be unknown to the Smritis ? As communities, they must have been in existence at the time of the Smritis. If they are Untouchables now, they must have been Untouchables then. Why then did the Smritis fail to mention them?

What about the third? If the Impure and the Untouchables are one and the same, why those communities which find a place in the Smritis do not find a place in the list given in the Order-in-Council? There are only two answers to this question. One is that though Untouchables at one time, they ceased to be Untouchables subsequently. The other is that the two lists contain names of communities who fall in altogether different categories. The first answer is untenable. For, Untouchability is permanent. Time cannot erase it or cleanse it. The only possible conclusion is the second.

Take the fourth. Why should Chamar alone find a place in the lists? The answer is not that the two lists include the same class of people. If it was the true answer, then not only the Chamar but all others included in the list given by the Smritis should appear in both the lists. But they do not. The true answer is that the two lists contain two different classes of people. The reason why some of those in the list of the Impure appear in the list of the Untouchables is that the Impure at one time became Untouchables. That the Chamar appears in both is far from being evidence to support the view that there is no difference between the Impure and the Untouchables. It proves that the Chamar who was at one time an Impure, subsequently became an Untouchable and had therefore to be included in both the lists. Of the twelve communities mentioned in the Smritis as Impure communities, only the Chamar should have been degraded to the status of an Untouchable is not difficult to explain. What has made the difference between the Chamar and the other impure communities is the fact of beef-eating. It is only those among the Impure who were eating beef that became Untouchables, when the cow became sacred and beef-eating became a sin. The Chamar is the only beef-eating community. That is why it alone appears in both the lists. The answer to the question relating to the Chamars is decisive on two points. It is conclusive on the point that the Impure are different from the Untouchables. It is also decisive on the point that it is beef-eating which is the root of Untouchability and which divides the Impure and the Untouchables.

The conclusion that Untouchability is not the same as Impurity has an important bearing on the determination of the date of birth of Untouchability. Without it any attempt at fixing the date would be missing the mark.

CHAPTER XVI

When did Broken Men become Untouchables ?

The foregoing researches and discussions have proved that there was a time when the village in India consisted of a Settled Community and Broken Men and that though both lived apart, the former inside the village and the latter outside it, there was no bar to social intercourse between the members of the Settled Community and the Broken Men. When the cow became sacred and beef-eating became taboo, society became divided into two - the Settled Community became a touchable community and Broken Men became an untouchable community. When did the Broken Men come to be regarded as Untouchables ? That is the last question that remains to be considered. There are obvious difficulties in the way of fixing a precise date for the birth of Untouchability. Untouchability is an aspect of social psychology. It is a sort of social nausea of one group against another group. Being an outgrowth of social psychology which must have taken some time to acquire form and shape, nobody can venture to fix a precise date to a phenomenon which probably began as a cloud no bigger than man's hand and grew till it took its final all-pervading shape as we know it today. When could the seed of Untouchability be said to have been sown? If it is not possible to fix an exact date, is it possible to fix an approximate date?

An exact date is not possible. But it is possible to give an approximate date. For this the first thing to do is to begin by fixing the upper time-limit at which Untouchability did not exist and the lower time-limit at which it had come into operation.

To begin with the question of fixing the upper limit the first thing to note is that those who are called Antyajas are mentioned in the Vedas. But they were not only not regarded as Untouchables but they were not even regarded as Impure. The following extract from Kane may be quoted in support of this conclusion. Says Kane[1].:

1 Dharma Shastra Vol II. Part I. p 165.

"In the early Vedic literature several of the names of castes that are spoken of in the Smritis as Antyajas occur. We have Carmanna (a tanner of hides) in the Rig Veda (VIII.8,38) the Chandala and Paulkasa occur in Vaj.S., the Vepa or Vapta (barber) even in the Rig., the Vidalakara or Bidalakar (corresponding to the Buruda of the Smritis) occurs in the Vaj.S. and the Tai.Br. Vasahpalpuli (washer woman) corresponding to the Rajakas of the Smritis in Vaj .S. But there is no indication in these passages whether they, even if they formed castes, were at all Untouchables."

Thus in Vedic times there was no Untouchability. As to the period of the Dharma Sutras, we have seen that there was Impurity but there was no Untouchability.

Was there Untouchability in the time of Manu? This question cannot be answered offhand. There is a passage[1] in which he says that there are only four varnas and that there is no fifth varna. The passage is enigmatical. It is difficult to make out what it means. Quite obviously the statement by Manu is an attempt by him to settle a controversy that must have been going on at the time he wrote. Quite obviously the controversy was about the status of a certain class in relation to the system of Chaturvarnya. Equally obvious is the point which was the centre of the controversy. To put briefly, the point was whether this class was to be deemed to be included within the Chaturvarnya or whether it was to be a fifth varna quite distinct from the original four varnas. All this is quite clear. What is, however, not clear is the class to which it refers. This is because Manu makes no specific mention of the class involved in the controversy.

The verse is also enigmatical because of the ambiguity in the decision given by Manu. Manu's decision is that there is no fifth varna. As a general proposition it has a meaning which everybody can understand. But what does this decision mean in the concrete application to the class whose status was the subject-matter of controversy. Obviously it is capable of two interpretations. It may mean that

1. Manu X. 4.

as according to the scheme of Chaturvarna there is no fifth varna the class in question must be deemed to belong to one of the four recognized varnas. But it may also mean that as in the original Varna System there is no provision for a fifth varna the class in question must be deemed to be outside the Varna System altogether.

The traditional interpretation adopted by the orthodox Hindu is that the statement in Manu refers to the Untouchables, that it was the Untouchables whose status was in controversy and that it was their status which is the subject-matter of Manu's decision. This interpretation is so firmly established that it has given rise to a division of Hindus into two classes called by different names, *Savarnas* or Hindus (those included in the Chaturvarna) and *Avarnas* or Untouchables (those excluded from the Chaturvarna). The question is, is this view correct ? To whom does the text refer ? Does it refer to the Untouchables ? A discussion of this question may appear to be out of place and remote from the question under consideration. But it is not so. For if the text does refer to the Untouchables then it follows that Untouchability did exist in the time of Manu—a conclusion which touches the very heart of the question under consideration. The matter must, therefore, be thrashed out.

I am sure this interpretation is wrong. I hold that the passage does not refer to the Untouchables at all. Manu does not say which was the fifth class whose status was in controversy and about whose status he has given a decision in this passage. Was it the class of Untouchables or was it some other class ? In support of my conclusion that the passage does not refer to Untouchables at all I rely on two circumstances. In the first place, there was no Untouchability in the time of Manu. There was only Impurity. Even the Chandala for whom Manu has nothing but contempt is only an impure person. That being so, this passage cannot possibly have any reference to Untouchables. In the second place, there is evidence to support the view that this passage has reference to slaves and not to Untouchables. This view is based on the language of the passage quoted from the Narada Smriti in the chapter on the Occupational Theory of Untouchability. It will be noticed that the Narada

Smriti speaks of the slaves as the fifth class. If the expression fifth class in the Narada Smriti refers to slaves, I see no reason why the expression fifth class in Manu Smriti should not be taken to have reference to slaves. If this reasoning is correct, it cuts at the very root of the contention that Untouchability existed in the time of Manu and that Manu was not prepared to include them as part of the Varna System. For the reasons stated, the passage does not refer to Untouchability and there is, therefore, no reason to conclude that there was Untouchability in the time of Manu.

Thus we can be sure of fixing the upper limit for the date of the birth of Untouchability. We can definitely say that Manu Smriti did not enjoin Untouchability. There, however, remains one important question. What is the date of Manu Smriti? Without an answer to this question it would not be possible for the average to relate the existence or non-existence of Untouchability to any particular point in time. There is no unanimity among savants regarding the date of Manu Smriti. Some regard it as very ancient and some regard it as very recent. After taking all facts into consideration Prof. Buhler has fixed a date which appears to strike the truth. According to Buhler, Manu Smriti in the shape in which it exists now, came into existence in the Second Century A.D.[1] In assigning so recent a date to the Manu Smriti Prof. Buhler is not quite alone. Mr. Daphtary has also come to the same conclusion. According to him Manu Smriti came into being after the year 185 B.C. and not before. The reason given by Mr. Daphtary is that Manu Smriti has a close connection with the murder of the Buddhist Emperor Brihadratha of the Maurya dynasty by his Brahmin Commander-in-Chief Pushyamitra Sunga and as even that took place in 185 B.C., he concludes that Manu Smriti must have been written after 185 B.C. To give support to so important a conclusion it is necessary to establish a nexus between the murder of Brihadratha Maurya by Pushyamitra and the writing of Manu Smriti by strong and convincing evidence. Mr. Daphatry has unfortunately omitted to do so. Consequently his conclusion appears to hang in the air. The establishment of such a

1. Buhler—Laws of Manu (S.B.E.) Vol. XXV. Int. CXN.

nexus is absolutely essential. Fortunately there is no want of evidence for the purpose.

The murder of Brihadratha Maurya by Pushyamitra has unfortunately passed unnoticed. At any rate it has not received the attention it deserves. It is treated by historians as an ordinary incident between two individuals as though its origin lay in some personal quarrel between the two. Having regard to its consequences it was an epoch-making event. Its significance cannot be measured by treating it as a change of dynasty—the Sungas succeeding the Mauryas. It was a political revolution as great as the French Revolution, if not greater. It was a revolution—a bloody revolution—engineered by the Brahmins to overthrow the rule of the Buddhist Kings. That is what the murder of Brihadratha by Pushyamitra means.

This triumphant Brahmanism was in need of many things. It of course needed to make Chaturvarna the law of the land the validity of which was denied by the Buddhists. It needed to make animal sacrifice, which was abolished by the Buddhists, legal. But it needed more than this. Brahmanism in bringing about this revolution against the rule of the Buddhist Kings had transgressed two rules of the customary law of the land which were accepted by all as sacrosanct and inviolable. The first rule made it a sin for a Brahmin even to touch a weapon. The second made the King's person sacred and regicide a sin. Triumphant Brahmanism wanted on a sacred text, infallible in its authority, to justify their transgressions. A striking feature of the Manu Smriti is that it not only makes Chaturvarna the law of the land; it not only makes animal sacrifice legal but it goes to state when a Brahmin could justifiably resort to arms and when he could justifiably kill the King. In this the Manu Smriti has done what no prior Smriti has done. It is a complete departure. It is a new thesis. Why should the Manu Smriti do this? The only answer is it had to strengthen the revolutionary deeds committed by Pushyamitra by propounding philosophic justification. This inter-connection between Pushya Mitra and the new thesis propounded by Manu shows that the Manu Smriti came into being some time after 185 B.C., a date not far removed from the date assigned by Prof. Buhler. Having got the date of the Manu Smriti we can say that in the Second Century A.D., there was no Untouchability.

Now to turn to the possibility of determining the lower limit to the birth of Untouchability. For this we must go to the Chinese travellers who are known to have visited India and placed on record what they saw of the modes and manners of the Indian people. Of these Chinese travellers Fah-Hian has something very interesting to say. He came to India in 400 A.D. In the course of his observations occurs the following passage[1] :—

> "Southward from this (Mathura) is the so-called middle-country (Madhyadesa). The climate of this country is warm and equable, without frost or snow. The people are very well off, without poll-tax or official restrictions. Only those who till the royal lands return a portion of profit of the land. If they desire to go, they go ; if they like to stop they stop. The kings govern without corporal punishment ; criminals are fined, according to circumstances, lightly or heavily. Even in cases of repeated rebellion they only cut off the right hand. The King's personal attendants, who guard him on the right and left, have fixed salaries. Throughout the country the people kill no living thing nor drink wine, nor do they eat garlic or onion, with the exception of Chandalas only. The Chandalas are named 'evil men' and dwell apart from others ; if they enter a town or market, they sound a piece of wood in order to separate themselves ; then, men knowing they are, avoid coming in contact with them. In this country they do not keep swine nor fowls, and do not deal in cattle ; they have no shambles or wine-shops in their market-places. In selling they use cowrie shells. The Chandalas only hunt and sell flesh."

Can this passage be taken as evidence of the prevalence of Untouchability at the time of Fah-Hian ? Certain parts of his description of the treatment given to the Chandalas

[1] Buddhist Records in Western India by Beal. Introduction p. xxxviii.

do seem to lend support to the conclusion, that is, a case of Untouchability.

There is, however, one difficulty in the way of accepting this conclusion. The difficulty arises because the facts relate to the Chandalas. The Chandalas is not a good case to determine the existence or non-existence of Untouchability. The Brahmins have regarded the Chandalas as their hereditary enemies and are prone to attribute to them abominable conduct ; hurl at them low epithets and manufacture towards them a mode of behaviour which is utterly artificial to suit their venom against them. Whatever, therefore, is said against the Chandalas must be taken with considerable reservations.

This argument is not based on mere speculation. Those who doubt its cogency may consider the evidence of Bana's Kadambari for a different description of the treatment accorded to the Chandalas.

The story of Kadambari is a very complex one and we are really not concerned with it. It is enough for our purpose to note that the story is told to King Shudraka by a parrot named Vaishampayana who was the pet of a Chandala girl. The following passages from the Kadambari are important for our purpose. It is better to begin with Bana's description of a Chandala settlement. It is in the following terms[1] :—

> "I beheld the barbarian settlement, a very market-place of evil deeds. It was surrounded on all sides by boys engaged in the chase, unleashing their hounds, teaching their falcons, mending snares, carrying weapons, and fishing, horrible in their attire, like demoniacs. Here and there the entrance to their dwellings, hidden by thick bamboo forests, was to be inferred, from the rising of smoke of orpiment. On all sides the enclosures were made with skulls ; (627) the dust-heaps on the roads were filled with bones ; the yards of the huts were miry with blood, fat, and meat chopped up. The life there consisted of hunting ; the food,

1. Kadambari (Ridding's Translation) p. 204.

> of flesh; the ointment, of fat; the garments, of coarse silk; the couches, of dried skins; the household attendants, of dogs; the animals for riding, of cows; the men's employment, of wine and women; the oblation to the gods, of blood; the sacrifice, of cattle. The place was the image of all hells."

It is from such a settlement that the Chandala girl starts with her parrot to the palace of King Shudraka. King Shudraka is sitting in the Hall of Audience with his Chieftains. A portress enters the Hall and makes the following announcement[1]:—

> "Sire, there stands at the gate a Candala maiden from the South, a royal glory of the race of that Tricamku who climbed the sky, but fell from it at the murder of wrathful Indra. She bears a parrot in a cage, and bids me thus hail your majesty: " Sire, thou, like the ocean, art alone worthy to receive the treasures of whole earth. In the thought that this bird is a marvel and the treasure of the whole earth, I bring it to lay at thy feet, and desire to behold thee," Thou, O king, hast heard her message, and must decide! so saying, she ended her speech. The king, whose curiosity was aroused, looked at the chiefs around him, and with the words 'Why not? Bid her enter' gave his permission.
> Then the portress, immediately on the king's order, ushered in the Candala maiden. And she entered."

The King and the Chieftains did not at first take notice of her. To attract attention she struck a bamboo on the mosaic floor to arouse the King. Bana then proceeds to desçribe her personal appearance.[2]

> "Then the king, with the words, 'Look yonder' to his suite, gazed steadily upon the Candala maiden, as she was pointed out by the portress. Before her went a man, whose hair was hoary

1. Kadambari (Ridding's Translation) p. 6.
2. Ibid pp 8-10.

with age, whose eyes were the colour of the red lotus, whose joints, despite the loss of youth, were firm from incessant labour, whose form, though that of Matanga, was not to be despised, and who wore the white raiment meet for a court. Behind her went a Candala boy, with locks falling on either shoulder, bearing a cage, the bars of which, though of gold. shone like emerald from the reflection of the parrot's plumage. She herself seemed by the darkness of her hue to imitate Krishna when he guilefully assumed a woman's attire to take away the amrita seized by the demons. She was, as it were, a doll of sapphire walking alone ; and over the blue garment, which reached to her ankle, there fell a veil of red silk, like evening sunshine falling on blue lotuses. The circle of her cheek was whitened by the ear-ring that hung from one ear, like the face of night inlaid with the rays of the rising moon ; she had a tawny tilaka of gorocana, as if it were a third eye, like Parvati in mountaineer's attire, after the fashion of the garb of Civa.

She was like Cri, darkened by the sapphire glory of Narayana reflected on the robe on her breast ; or like Rati, stained by smoke which rose as Madana was burnt by the fire of wrathful Civa ; or like Yamuna, fleeing in fear of being drawn along by the ploughshare of wild Balarama ; or, from the rich lac that turned her lotus feet into budding shoots, like Durga, with her feet crimsoned by the blood of the Asura Mahisha she had just trampled upon.

Her nails were rosy from the pink glow of her fingers ; the mosaic pavement seemed too hard for her touch, and she came forward. placing her feet like tender twigs upon the ground.
The rays of her anklets, rising in flame-colour, seemed to encircle her as with the arms of Agni. as though, by his love for her beauty, he would

purify the stain of her birth, and so set the Creator at naught.

Her girdle was like the stars wreathed on the brow of the elephant of Love ; and her necklace was a rope of large bright pearls, like the stream of Ganga just tinged by Yamuna.

Like autumn, she opened her lotus eyes ; like the rainy season, she had cloudy tresses ; like the circle of the Malaya Hills, she was wreathed with sandal ; like the zodiac, she was decked with starry gems ; like Cri, she had the fairness of a lotus in her hand ; like a swoon, she entranced the heart ; like a forest, she was endowed with living beauty ; like the child of a goddess, she was claimed by no tribe ; like sleep, she charmed the eyes ; as a lotus-pool in a wood is troubled by elephants, so was she dimmed by her Matanga birth ; like spirit, she might not be touched ; like a letter, she gladdened the eyes alone ; like the blossoms of spring she lacked the jati flower ; her slender waist, like the line of Love's bow, could be spanned by the hands ; with her curly hair, she was like the Lakshmi of the Yaksha king in Alaka. She had but reached the flower of her youth, and was beautiful exceedingly. And the king was amazed ; and the thought arose in his mind, 'Ill-placed was the labour of the Creator in producing this beauty ! For if she has been created as though in mockery of her Candala form, such that all the world's wealth of loveliness is laughed to scorn by her own, why was she born in a race with which none can mate ? Surely by thought alone did Prajapati create her, fearing the penalties of contact with the Matanga race, else whence this unsullied radiance, a grace that belongs not to limbs sullied by touch ? Moreover, though fair in form, by the basenness of her birth, whereby she, like a Lakshmi of the lower world, is a perpetual reproach to the gods, she, lovely as she is, causes fear in Brahma, the maker of so strange a union.' While the king was thus thinking the maiden, garlanded with flowers, that fell over her ears, bowed herself before him with a confidence beyond her years. And when she had made her reverence and stepped on to the mosaic floor, her attendant, taking the parrot, which had just entered the cage, advanced a few steps and, showing it to the King, said: 'Sire, this parrot, by name Vaicampayana, knows the meaning of all the castras, is expert in the practice of royal policy, skilled in tales, history, and Puranas, and acquainted with songs and with musical intervals. He recites, and himself composes graceful and incomparable modern romances, love-stories, plays, and poems, and the like; he is versed in witticisms and is an unrivalled disciple of the vina, flute, and drum. He is skilled in displaying the different movements of dancing, dextrous in painting, very bold in play, ready in resources to calm a maiden angered in a lover's quarrel, and familiar with the characteristics of elephants, horses, men, and women. He is the gem of the whole earth; and in the thought that treasures belong to thee, as pearls to the ocean, the daughter of my lord has brought him hither to thy feet, O king! Let him be accepted as thine.'

On reading this description of a Chandala girl many questions arise. Firstly, how different it is from the description given by Fa-Hian? Secondly Bana is a Vatsyayana Brahmin. This Vatsyayana Brahmin, after giving a description of the Chandala Settlement, finds no compunction in using such eloquent and gorgeous language to describe the Chandala girl. Is this description compatible with the sentiments of utter scorn and contempt associated with Untouchability? If the Chandalas were Untouchables how could an Untouchable girl enter the King's palace? How could an Untouchable be described in the superb terms used by Bana? Far from being degraded, the Chandalas of Bana's period had Ruling Families among them.

For Bana speaks of the Chandala girl as a Chandala princess[1]. Bana wrote some time about 600 A.D. and by 600 A.D. the Chandalas had not come to be regarded as Untouchables. It is, therefore, quite possible that the conditions described by Fa-Hian, though bordering on Untouchability, may not be taken as amounting to Untouchability. It may only be extreme form of impurity practised by the Brahmins who are always in the habit of indulging in overdoing their part in sacerdotalism. This becomes more than plausible if we remember that when Fa-Hian came to India it was the reign of the Gupta Kings The Gupta Kings were patrons of Brahmanism. It was a period of the triumph and revival of Brahmanism, It is quite possible that what Fa-Hian describes is not Untouchability but an extremity to which the Brahmins were prepared to carry the ceremonial impurity which had become attached to some community, particularly to the Chandalas.

The next Chinese traveller who came into India was Yuan Chwang. He came to India in 629 A.D. He stayed in India for 16 years and has left most accurate records of journeys up and down the country and of the manners and customs of the people. In the course of his description of general characters of the cities and buildings of India, he says[2] :—

> "As to their inhabited towns and cities the quadrangular walls of the cities (or according to one text, of the various regions) are broad and high, while the thoroughfares are narrow tortuous passages. The shops are on the highways and booths, or (inns) line the roads. Butchers, fishermen, public performers, executioners, and scavengers have their habitations marked by a distinguishing sign. They are forced to live outside the city and they sneak along on the left when going about in the hamlets."

The above passage is too short and too brief for founding a definite conclusion thereon. There is, however, one

1. Kadambari (Ridding's Translation) p. 204.

2. Walters-Yuan Chwang Vol. I. p. 147.

point about it which is worthy of note. Fa-Hian's description refers to the Chandalas only while the description given by Yuan Chwang applies to communities other than the Chandalas. This is a point of great impórtance. No such argument can be levelled against the acceptance of a description since it applies to communities other than the Chandalas. It is, therefore. just possible that when Yuan Chwang came to India, Untouchability had emerged.

On the basis of what has been said above we can conclude that while Untouchability did not exist in 200 A.D, it had emerged by 600 A.D.

These are the two limits, upper and lower, for determining the birth of Untouchability. Can we fix an approximate date for the birth of Untouchability ? I think we can, if we take beef-eating, which is the root of Untouchability, as the point to start from. Taking the ban on beef-eating as a point to reconnoitre from, it follows that the date of the birth of Untouchability must be intimately connected with the ban on cow-killing and on eating beef. If we can answer when cow-killing became an offence and beef-eating became a sin, we can fix an approximate date for the birth of Untouchability.

When did cow-killing become an offence ?

We know that Manu did not prohibit the eating of beef nor did he make cow-killing an offence. When did it become an offence? As has been shown by Dr. D R. Bhandarkar, cow killing was made a capital offence by the Gupta kings some time in the 4th Century A.D.

We can, therefore, say with some confidence that Untouchability was born some time about 400 A.D. It is born out of the struggle for supremacy between Buddhism and Brahmanism which has so completely moulded the history of India and the study of which is so woefully neglected by students of Indian history.

THE END

INDEX

T

U

V

W

Y